The Behavior *Shift*: A Roadmap to Understanding and Shaping Behavior

Regina Christian-Massey

Faith-Informed | Trauma-Aware | Evidence-Based

Copyright © 2023 Teacher Mod Squad
All rights reserved.

The Behavior Shift: A Roadmap to Understanding and Shaping Behavior

Copyright © 2023 All rights reserved. No part of this publication may be reproduced, distributed, or transmitted in any form or by any means, including photocopying, recording, or other electronic or mechanical methods, without the prior written permission of the publisher, except in the case of brief quotations embodied in critical reviews and certain other noncommercial uses permitted by copyright law. For permission requests, write to the publisher, addressed "Attention: Permissions Coordinator," at the email address below.

Teacher Mod Squad, LLC
teachermodsquad@yahoo.com
www.teachermodsquad.com

ISBN: 978-0-9704215-4-8

Ordering Information:

Quantity sales. Special discounts are available on quantity purchases by schools, corporations, associations, and others. For details, contact the publisher at the address above.

Printed in the United States of America

Published by Teacher Mod Squad
All rights reserved

DEDICATION

To the educators and mentors who shape young minds, equipping them with tools to navigate the complexities of human interactions, your guidance and wisdom lay the foundation for a brighter, more empathetic world. Thank you for courageously embarking on your journey of self-reflection and growth, striving to better understand your impact on the world. Thank you for your desire to increase your capacity, remain open-minded, and your commitment to adopting new processes that can yield better results in your classrooms. It is essential to recognize that you are the experts in your classrooms, and your expertise is invaluable in creating a safe space for students to develop into well-rounded young adults.

To my family, your patience, compassion, and unwavering support create a sanctuary for my continued development and birthing of new ideas. This dedication is a tribute to you and all those who believe in the power of knowledge, spirituality, and self-discovery. Together, we can create a world where understanding and empathy reign while leading to accountability.

Prayer of Gratitude

In moments of uncertainty, Lord, you have provided me with clarity in this project. When faced with challenges, you have given me the resilience and perseverance to overcome them. Your divine inspiration has ignited my creativity and fueled my motivation, enabling me to produce my best work.

I acknowledge that without your presence and leadership, I would not have been able to accomplish this project with such success. You have been my rock, guiding light, and source of inspiration. I am humbled and grateful for your solace and forethought in my life.

Thank you, Father, for your love, patience, and grace. I am eternally grateful for your blessings and for your presence. May *The Behavior Shift* serve as a testament to your greatness, and may it bring glory to your name.

In Your Service,
Amen

Foreword

Having spent over twenty-five years as a licensed social worker providing therapy and counseling to children and families in their homes, in schools and in the community, I found myself teaching counseling and human relation courses at Atlanta Christian College (Point University) in Atlanta, Georgia. This is where I met Regina Christian. She was enrolled in a non-traditional program designed for working adults. Regina epitomized the type of student this program was designed for. She was serious about her education, determined to complete the program and highly motivated.

When she asked me to provide a foreword for *The Behavior Shift: A Roadmap to Understanding and Shaping Behavior*, I was humbled. I knew and understood that this was not just another book about working with children with behavior problems. That it was at its heart, a ministry of sorts designed to transform the lives of both students and educators through a greater understanding of how spirituality can inform and enrich the educational experience of these children.

The *Behavior Shift* provides a look into the role that spirituality has in understanding and addressing behavior and why it is important to this discussion. It opens by introducing the reader to a young lady named Christin who is struggling with several emotional and behavioral problems that have deeply impacted her life experience. It then takes the reader on a journey of discovery into understanding human behavior, intervention tools and techniques, practices, and protocols.

Spirituality is defined and discussed in practical terms and in relation to education. Psychosocial approaches to behavior management are discussed and practical applications are provided using real-life scenarios. The *Behavior Shift* challenges readers to consider not only the role that spirituality has in their work with children, but also in their own lives. Although written from a Christian world view, its tenets are true for all faith traditions. It recognizes that spirituality is not the solution to behavior problems but in a system that frequently struggles with the separation of church and state, it asserts that it should be considered in the address of the problem. The *Behavior Shift* is prescribing a paradigm shift. A change in the way we see and address the behavior of children that is inclusive of spirituality.

The *Behavior Shift* does not leave us hanging about what happens to Christin. The rest of Christin's story is revealed at the end.

Dr. Shirley Thompson-Lewis

Assistant Professor of Human Relations and Social Work, Field Education Director, Point University (Dept. Sociology and Social Work)

Acknowledgements

Writing a book is never a solitary endeavor. It requires the support, guidance, and contributions of numerous individuals who have pivotal roles in its creation. As I reflect upon the completion of *The Behavior Shift: A Roadmap to Understanding and Shaping Behavior,* I am filled with deep gratitude for those who have been instrumental in bringing this work to fruition.

I thank my family for your persistent encouragement, understanding, and patience. Your belief in me and my passion for helping shape young adults has always inspired me to seek much-needed change.

I feel a strong sense of appreciation for friends and colleagues who have provided invaluable feedback. Your diverse perspectives, stimulating discussions, and thoughtful input have greatly enriched the content of this book. Your willingness to engage in meaningful conversations and share your expertise has helped shape my ideas.

Lastly, I extend my heartfelt gratitude to the readers of this book. It is for you that *The Behavior Shift* was written. The insights shared within these pages will empower you to understand and shape behavior, leading to positive changes in your lives and those around you.

Thank you,

Regina

A ROADMAP TO UNDERSTANDING AND SHAPING BEHAVIOR

A ROADMAP TO UNDERSTANDING AND SHAPING BEHAVIOR

Table of Contents

The Awakening — 1

Introduction — 3

Recognizing The Interplay Of Spirituality and Behavior

Chapter 1: — 9

The Role of Spirituality in Behavior

Chapter 2: — 15

Nature v/s Nurture

Chapter 3: — 25

Transforming Perspectives: Mindsets Have Power

Chapter 4: — 33

Cultivating Compassion through Spiritual Practices

Chapter 5: — 39

Mindfulness and its Connection to Behavior

Chapter 6: — 43

Mindfulness-Based Behavior Modification Techniques

Chapter 7: 51

Integrating Ethical Considerations into Behavioral Management

Chapter 8: 57

Evidenced Based Strategies

Chapter 9: 61

Effective Communication and Active Listening

Chapter 10: 65

Understanding Challenging Behaviors

Chapter 11: 71

Integrating Emotional Regulation Techniques

Chapter 12: 75

Understanding the Significance of Trauma

Chapter 13: 79

Healing, Restoration, and Resilience

Chapter 14: 83

Recognizing and Respecting Cultural Differences

Chapter 15: 87

The Role of Functional Behavior Assessments

Chapter 16: 93

Application: Real-Life Scenarios

Chapter 17: 99

The Unveiling: A Journey of Healing & Hope

Final Thoughts 103

References 105

About the Author 115

A ROADMAP TO UNDERSTANDING AND SHAPING BEHAVIOR

The Awakening

In a small, ordinary classroom, Christin sat fidgeting in her social studies class, her stomach twisting into knots. It was just another mundane day in high school, but today was different. Today, a profound realization was bubbling within her, like a whisper deep within her soul. She had been grappling with her identity, torn between the advice of the adults in her life and the desire for something more.

As she looked out of the classroom window, her thoughts swirled. She yearned for happiness, a respite from the overwhelming hopelessness that had clung to her like a shadow. Three years ago, at the tender age of 12, her world shattered when her mother's abusive boyfriend tore apart the only home she had ever known.

In the wake of the trauma, Christin had experienced spells of anger and resentment, blaming everyone for the chaos that had consumed her family and her life. At 15, she was a different person, a young woman weighed down by mental health issues stemming from her turbulent past. The school had become a battleground, and her aggression toward the staff reflected the turmoil within.

Her psychologist recognized her potential and intellectual gifts, but the trauma had cast a long shadow, making it difficult for her to thrive in a general education classroom without support. She had been diagnosed with post-traumatic stress disorder, clinical depression, anxiety, and intermittent explosive disorder. Christin's life seemed to be a relentless cycle of chaos, school troubles, and an overwhelming sense of despair. In her darkest moments, Christin confided in her therapist, revealing that her outbursts were not acts of defiance but cries of pain and frustration. She carried her hurt and fear like a weighted blanket, suffocating her spirit.

Desperation led Christin down a different path. She turned to faith, seeking solace in the scriptures. A verse from Philippians 4:13 became her guiding light: "I can do all things through Him who strengthens me." and Jeremiah 3:11, "For I know the plans I have for you,' declares the Lord, 'plans to prosper you and not to harm you, plans to give you a hope and a future." This newfound spirituality breathed life into her weary soul. At the advice of her therapist, she began to embrace the power of Cognitive Behavioral Therapy

(CBT). This tool helped her challenge the negative thought patterns that had held her captive. Her spirit was soothed, and her anxiety lessened through mindfulness and daily meditation.

With time, Christin's determination and newfound faith began to bring a sense of balance to her life. The darkness that had once engulfed her began to recede, replaced by a glimmer of hope. She discovered her spiritual purpose, allowing her to heal some of the deep emotional wounds that had scarred her. Slowly but steadily, she rebuilt her relationships with others, showing that there was potential for growth and recovery even in the most difficult times. This was the beginning of Christin's journey, a testament to the profound role that spirituality would play in shaping her life and behavior.

Introduction

Recognizing The Interplay Of Spirituality and Behavior

In matters of behavior ... less focus on control and more focus on change.

The Essence of Spirituality in Education

Education has long been recognized as having many aspects that extend beyond mere knowledge transfer from teacher to student. Although academic excellence remains a priority, educators increasingly acknowledge the significance of fostering personal growth, well-being, and the development of values and character in students. One often-underexplored dimension of education that can impact these aspects is spirituality. *The Behavior Shift* delves into spirituality from the Christian perspective.

Spirituality is a complex concept encompassing a range of beliefs, practices, and experiences. It is inherently about a connection to something greater than oneself, which can manifest in various ways, including religious beliefs, mindfulness practices, ethical principles, and a sense of interconnectedness. In education, spirituality may be understood as the pursuit of meaning, purpose, and the development of values and ethics. It is not limited to religious beliefs but includes a broader quest for personal and collective well-being.

When integrating spirituality into education, it is important to consider students' diverse cultural and religious backgrounds. The approach should be inclusive, respecting the beliefs and values of all students. The process can be transformative to their learning experiences and enhance their well-being. Moreover, educators should receive appropriate training to facilitate discussions on spirituality and to ensure that it is integrated into the curriculum sensitively and respectfully.

While challenges exist in navigating students' diverse beliefs and backgrounds, a thoughtful and inclusive approach can yield substantial benefits in pursuing holistic education. The essence of spirituality is highly individual, and it may manifest differently for each person. It is a dynamic and evolving aspect of the human experience that can guide individuals on their journey toward meaning, purpose, and well-being.

The concept of "God's word" refers to the teachings, principles, and spiritual guidance found in revered texts such as the Bible, Quran, Torah, or other sacred scriptures, depending on one's faith. These texts are believed by many to contain divine revelations or instructions from a higher power, thus connecting them to how we interact with the world around us. For people who follow a particular religious faith, God's word plays a central role in shaping their behavior and moral values. It provides a framework and guidelines for how believers should conduct themselves, interact with others, and make ethical decisions. The teachings within these religious texts often address various aspects of human behavior, including personal conduct, relationships, justice, compassion, and societal responsibilities.

When individuals follow their religious teachings, moral and ethical principles, they may work to align their actions and attitudes with these beliefs. By doing so, they can promote honesty, kindness, forgiveness, empathy, humility, and love for others, which can ultimately influence their behavior. A religious person may view God's word as a source of authority, guiding them to live by what they perceive as divine will. They may believe that obedience to these teachings leads to personal growth and spiritual fulfillment. Belief in a higher power contributes to a harmonious and just society.

It is important to note that interpretations of God's word may change among differing religious communities. It is essential to recognize that cultural context, personal beliefs, and the influence of religious leaders all have a substantial role in how individuals interpret and apply teachings to their lives. By understanding these factors, we can gain a deeper appreciation for the diversity of perspectives that exist within our communities. We must approach these conversations confidently and with an open-mind, striving to learn and grow alongside those around us.

Shaping behavior is a complex process involving understanding human psychology, motivations, and the factors influencing our actions. There is no one-size-fits-all roadmap, as behavior is influenced by individual differences and the specific context in which it occurs. As someone who has spent my career in some facet of education and leadership, and as a person of faith, I firmly believe in the power of a higher being. Especially in today's world, where the teaching profession is facing many challenges, it is crucial to tap into spiritual resources to help guide and support us in our work with students. If we seek guidance, God will give us wisdom and knowledge to equip us for this calling.

Incorporating spirituality into our behavior management approach can profoundly impact students' lives and help them develop into responsible, compassionate individuals. It is a topic that warrants further discussion and exploration within the educational community. Spirituality is an incredibly powerful force that can profoundly affect our lives and shape the essence of who we are at our core. It is all about forming a deep connection with something greater than ourselves, whether that is a higher power, the universe, or simply a sense of purpose and meaning. Moreover, while spirituality is a deeply personal experience, it can shape our behavior in countless ways. There are five key areas of spirituality that I feel are particularly important as we discuss shaping behavior:

1. Values and Ethics

Spirituality connects to a set of values and ethical principles that guide actions in life. As a moral compass, spirituality profoundly influences behavior, fostering integrity, forgiveness, and deep-rooted respect for others. Individuals firmly rooted in their spirituality place great importance on empathy, social justice, and the overall welfare of fellow beings. Consequently, their behavior is shaped by these values, leading them to engage in actions that are marked by compassion and ethical conduct.

2. Meaning and Purpose

Spirituality can bestow individuals with a feeling of direction and purpose in life. When individuals have a solid grasp of their core values and feel connected to something greater than themselves, they often experience an overwhelming sense of satisfaction and fulfillment. This feeling of purpose can motivate people to make choices and take actions that align with their spiritual beliefs, like showing kindness, generosity, and serving others.

3. Emotional Well-being

Spirituality can greatly impact our emotional well-being. We can achieve inner harmony and contentment despite difficulties by incorporating practices like prayer, meditation, or reflection. By developing a positive outlook through spiritual practices, we can also promote self-control, resilience, and the ability to respond to challenging situations with patience and a sense of peace.

4. Interpersonal Relationships

Spirituality possesses the potential to nurture affirmative relationships and exert a considerable influence on behavior within social settings. Numerous spiritual practices prioritize the significance of love, compassion, and establishing meaningful connections with others. By wholeheartedly embracing these principles, individuals are more inclined to exhibit prosocial behaviors, including empathizing with others, embracing forgiveness, and actively facilitating harmony within their relationships. Additionally, spirituality offers a sense of belonging to a community or religious group, thereby shaping behavior through shared values and collective engagement in rituals or traditions.

5. Self-Reflection/Personal Growth

Spirituality frequently encompasses the practice of self-reflection, introspection, and an inherent drive for personal development. By engaging in meditation, contemplation, or journaling, individuals can gain rich insight into themselves, their thoughts, and their behaviors. This heightened level of self-awareness holds the potential for profound personal transformation and catalyzes behavioral shifts as we actively seek to align our actions with our spiritual aspirations.

Spirituality is a unique and deeply personal concept, and its influence on behavior can differ greatly from person to person. While it can undoubtedly spark positive change, it is important to acknowledge that it can also be wielded as a tool to justify harmful actions, depending on how it is interpreted and applied. Therefore, it is crucial to approach spirituality and its impact on behavior with a comprehensive understanding of the broader context and other factors that shape an individual's actions.

"To navigate the complex interplay between spirituality and challenging behaviors effectively, educators, counselors, and researchers can adopt practical recommendations" (Hamric & Wocial, 2016). These include conducting comprehensive assessments to tailor individualized support, fostering culturally and spiritually inclusive education environments, implementing mindfulness and social-emotional learning programs incorporating spirituality, providing educators with professional development opportunities, and encouraging collaborative efforts among stakeholders. By following these steps, we can establish an educational environment that is more inclusive, supportive and respectful of the potential of spirituality in addressing challenging student behaviors.

Chapter 1:

THE ROLE OF SPIRITUALITY IN BEHAVIOR

Spiritual beliefs have the power to guide the heart, nurture compassion, and enrich the tapestry of education.

The role of spirituality in behavior can differ considerably depending on an individual's beliefs, cultural context, and personal experiences. Different spiritual traditions and practices may emphasize different aspects and have unique effects on shaping behavior. Furthermore, spirituality is not the sole determinant of behavior, as other factors like upbringing, social influences, and individual differences also play fundamental roles. We often connect spirituality to our search for meaning, purpose, and connection to something greater than ourselves. According to the Bible, knowing God is the meaning of life, because He is the "author of life" (John 17:3). Searching for the meaning of life is not based on things we see in the world "for life is more than food, and the body more than clothing" (Luke 12:23, KJB, 2017).

Given this understanding, spirituality could influence behavior in various ways, some directly and others indirectly. Nevertheless, we are directly impacted when we go through the process of Self-Reflection or Self-Development. Many spiritual traditions emphasize self-reflection, introspection, and personal growth. Engaging in meditation, prayer, or mindfulness practices can help with awareness of thoughts, emotions, and behaviors. This self-awareness can lead to greater self-control, emotional regulation, and the ability to make intentional choices about one's behavior. Colossians 3:23 reminds us, "Whatever you do, work heartily, as for the Lord and not for men."

How we cope with challenges is often dictated by our self-awareness. Spirituality can provide us with a source of comfort, solace, and resilience in times of difficulty or stress. Spiritual practices, rituals, or beliefs can offer hope, meaning, and support. These practices may impact behavior by enabling us to cope with challenges in healthier ways, such as seeking social support, practicing forgiveness, or finding gratitude under challenging circumstances.

The Bible reminds us in Matthew 5:16 (KJB, 2017), "In the Christian way, let your light shine before others, so that they may see your good works and give glory to your Father who is in heaven." How we think is critical in making behavior modifications. A negative mindset can cause our ability to change to stagnate. Spirituality often encourages positive mindsets and attitudes, such as gratitude, acceptance, and mindfulness. These perspectives can influence behavior by promoting optimism, resilience, and a focus on personal growth. They can also contribute to a more positive interpersonal approach, leading to healthier relationships and constructive interactions.

Throughout this book, you will be reminded that teachers can and should foster a safe and supportive atmosphere in which students feel comfortable expressing their beliefs and values. When teachers incorporate mindfulness and meditation practices into their curriculum, it helps students develop a more profound sense of self-awareness and self-control. Teachers can model positive behaviors and attitudes that align with spiritual values, such as compassion, forgiveness, and gratitude. This may inspire students to adopt these Christiane values and behaviors in their own lives, both in and out of the classroom.

Exploring the Impact of Spiritual Beliefs on Education

In Engel v. Vitale, 370 U.S. 421 (1962), the Supreme Court ruled that school-sponsored prayer in public schools violated the First Amendment's establishment clause (kembrel.com). While the Constitution says the government cannot establish a religion, it also says that it cannot inhibit religious freedom — a provision that allows students, and to a lesser degree, teachers, to express their faith openly in school. There are many pros and cons to the ruling of 1962. However, its removal cannot change belief systems taught and nurtured by parents and guardians alike at an early age. This system often serves as the foundation for entering education and the expectations or limitations of each educator's practices.

The following passage found in *Sincerely Held Beliefs* (1994, 2022), warns us about the unintended consequences of limiting religious expressions and teachings in public schools in the name of religious liberty. It argues that such restrictions might lead religious communities to establish their own schools, which could have negative consequences for public schools.

> If the Court in the name of religious liberty tries to keep a lid on religious expression and teaching both in the public school and also in connection with experiments that involve cooperation with the public school, it will drive all religious communities to the establishment of parochial schools, much against the will of many, and to the great detriment of public schools and probably of the quality of education

(Dills, Norton, 2022).

The author noted a shift towards parochial schools could harm public schools as they could lose students and resources, potentially leading to a decline in the quality of education the public school can provide its community.

The First Amendment

In the United States, the First Amendment to the U.S. Constitution includes a clause that states, "Congress shall make no law respecting an establishment of religion, or prohibiting the free exercise thereof." This clause is often interpreted as establishing a separation of church and state in the U.S., meaning the government may not promote or favor any particular religion. This principle has been the basis for many court decisions and legal precedents in the United States. In an educational context, this often means that public schools, which the government funds, should not promote or endorse any particular religion and should provide a secular education that respects their students' diverse beliefs and backgrounds.

Research shows that the absence of religion in schools can create a more inclusive and unbiased learning environment. It allows for focusing on secular education, emphasizing science, mathematics, literature, and history without religious bias. This absence promotes respect for different beliefs and can provide a better learning experience for students from diverse religious backgrounds or those who do not adhere to any particular religion (Lupu et al., 2019).

However, the absence of religious instruction in schools can also have drawbacks. It can lead to confusion regarding ethical education, as alternative approaches to ethics and morality without religious instruction may not align with parental ethics and values. Additionally, limiting access to religious teaching may reduce understanding of religious traditions' historical, cultural, and artistic significance, which has played a critical role in shaping human history, art, literature, and societal norms.

To create an inclusive and unbiased learning environment that respects and accommodates the diverse spiritual beliefs of students and the community, educators should be aware of the potential influence of religious or spiritual values on teaching, curriculum, student well-being, and the overall educational environment. Educators may consider allowing students to explore their beliefs and experiences within a self-discovery framework, emphasizing critical thinking and open dialogue rather than promoting a particular moral stance. This will provide opportunities for them to reflect on their values and beliefs without imposing any particular ideology. Teachers and students may focus on authentic behavioral changes by discussing ethical principles, moral dilemmas, and values found across various belief systems. Emphasizing critical thinking and open dialogue rather than promoting a particular moral stance allows students to engage in what is morally and ethically acceptable regarding their behavior.

With the current critical state of education, particularly due to behavior and mental health issues, it is crucial that we recognize the need for change. By incorporating students' belief systems into behavioral expectations, ethical standards, or working with integrity, we may be able to make a significant difference in our classrooms. We must recognize that our students have diverse religious backgrounds. Acknowledging their beliefs creates an inclusive and supportive learning environment. Learning about their spiritual beliefs can also help us understand their values, morals, and perspectives and elevate their educational experience. Moreover, incorporating spirituality into the curriculum can promote mindfulness, empathy, and a sense of purpose among students. It is our responsibility to create a safe space, ensure that others respect that space, and make sure that students feel comfortable expressing their beliefs and engaging in meaningful discussions.

Chapter 2:

Nature v/s Nurture

Spirituality shapes us; while nature and nurture influence us, they do not dictate our actions.

Discovering spirituality is a journey that has no age limit. It is never too late for individuals or families to embark on this path, even if they have never attended church or engaged in religious practices. Spirituality is a deeply personal and flexible concept that can be nurtured and explored at any stage in life. To tap into faith and connect with one's inner spirituality, individuals and families can begin with self-reflection to identify their values, beliefs, and questions about the meaning of life. Exploring different faith traditions, philosophical teachings, or personal philosophies can provide insight and inspiration.

Spirituality plays a significant role in shaping who we are as individuals. While nature and nurture contribute to our development, spirituality adds a unique dimension to our lives. It serves as the foundation of our values, instilling morality, compassion, and love for others, which shapes our character. Spirituality also provides a sense of purpose and meaning, guiding us toward positive behaviors that align with our beliefs. It fosters resilience, enabling us to navigate challenges and maintain a positive outlook. These elements shape our character and guide our actions, especially in our younger years, but essentially throughout our lives.

As a powerful catalyst, spirituality or faith can promote personal growth and transformation. As individuals and families delve into their spirituality, they often find a greater sense of purpose, inner peace, and an increased focus on values that promote positive behavior change. Embracing this concept can fortify acts of kindness, empathy, and a deeper sense of community, all of which can lead to meaningful shifts in behavior, even if one has never attended a traditional sanctuary.

When we introduce faith early on it can have a significant impact on adolescents' development. However, in their natural curiosity and openness to learning, young people absorb the values and beliefs of their surroundings whether from school or within their community. To effectively convey spiritual concepts to children, age-appropriate language and activities are key. Stories, parables, and interactive discussions can be great tools to communicate complex spiritual ideas in ways that children can understand and relate to. Ultimately, this child-focused approach empowers the next generation to lead virtuous and fulfilling lives rooted in their faith and spiritual beliefs, setting them on a path of purpose, meaning, and positive behavior.

Nature, Nurture, & Individual Change (Mullen, 2006) noted therapists have sought change in the behaviors and attitudes of their clients, individuals attempt the Christiane on their own, and parents seek to instill personal traits in their developing children. In all these cases the intention is to alter either what already is or what is thought likely to develop. One issue that has been considered to be relevant to these attempts at individual change is whether the behaviors and traits are more a result of nature or nurture. On the nature side, some argue that spirituality may have a biological basis, suggesting that certain genetic factors could predispose individuals to be more receptive to spiritual experiences or beliefs. On the nurture side, the environment in which individuals are raised can significantly impact their spiritual development. Cultural, familial, and societal influences can shape one's beliefs, values, and understanding of spirituality.

The nature vs. nurture debate is a fundamental discussion in psychology that revolves around the relative contributions of genetics (nature) and the environment (nurture) in shaping human behavior and development. Both nature and nurture play significant roles in influencing behavior. Genetics provide individuals with a biological foundation, determining traits and predispositions. Meanwhile, the environment, encompassing family, culture, upbringing, and life experiences, exerts a powerful influence on behavior by shaping an individual's values, beliefs, and social interactions.

While genetics may set certain boundaries, it is nurture, the environmental influences, that often holds the key to changing one's behavior. The interplay between nature and nurture allows for the possibility of behavioral change through environmental interventions, therapy, and personal growth. Research has consistently demonstrated the potential for individuals to modify their behavior through learned behaviors, therapy, and personal development.

Research in this field has shown that the impact of nurture can be profound. For instance, studies have illustrated how interventions like cognitive-behavioral therapy can help individuals overcome destructive behaviors or emotional challenges. Additionally, the impact of early childhood experiences on adult behavior and mental health has been extensively documented (Firpo-Cappiello, 2020). The relationship between nature vs. nurture and spirituality is complex. Some argue that spirituality may have a genetic component, making it part of an individual's nature, while others maintain that it is primarily a product of upbringing and cultural influences, thus falling under the domain of nurture. However, it is important to recognize that spirituality can be a deeply personal and individual experience, shaped by both genetic predispositions and environmental factors.

The interplay between nature and nurture continues throughout one's life and can influence personal interactions. While early experiences can have a profound impact, individuals remain capable of change and growth at any age. Personal development and behavioral changes can occur even in adulthood, reflecting the ongoing dynamic between nature and nurture. Research has shown that nurturing, learning, and therapeutic interventions can contribute to significant changes in behavior, providing hope for personal growth and transformation (Kirby, 2020).

IMPACT OF ENVIRONMENT ON BEHAVIOR

Studies suggest that the environment plays a crucial role in shaping the inherent characteristics of children (Sholikhah et al., 2019). Although the environment establishes a foundation, individuals have the capacity to actively adjust, oppose, or modify their behavior through personal experiences, values, contexts, and motivations. The biblical passage from Romans 12:2 (KJB, 2017) encourages individuals not to conform blindly to the societal norms or behaviors commonly found in the world. Instead, it advises a transformative process that involves renewing one's mind. By doing so, individuals gain the ability to discern and align themselves with what is considered God's will; something described as good, pleasing, and perfect.

When applied to children with challenging behaviors, this biblical advice can be interpreted in a way that suggests fostering a transformative approach to their conduct. Rather than conforming to negative patterns or behaviors prevalent in their environment, the emphasis is on promoting a renewal of mindset. This may involve helping children understand and internalize positive values, moral principles, and healthier ways of interacting with others.

In practical terms, this could involve educational and therapeutic interventions that aim to transform the underlying thought patterns and emotional responses contributing to challenging behaviors. By renewing their minds, children may develop a greater capacity to make choices aligned with values that are positive, pleasing, and conducive to their overall well-being. The goal is not to conform to negative patterns but to undergo a positive transformation that leads to improved behavior and a more fulfilling life.

The environment, particularly during childhood, is crucial for shaping behavior and socialization practices. "Train up a child in the way he should go; even when he is old, he will not depart from it" (Proverbs 22:6, KJB). Individuals learn behavioral norms, values, and beliefs through interactions with family, peers, and other social institutions. These social interactions heavily influence one's behavior and shape attitudes and perspectives. When looking at the whole child, we must explore family influence, cultural norms, community, socio-economic status, education, and experiences, as they all contribute to molding an individual's thoughts, attitudes, and behavior. In addition, the effects of trauma and adversity can have long term and negative impacts on an individual. Negative childhood experiences, such as abuse or neglect, can have lasting effects on behavior, leading to various social, emotional, and behavioral issues later in life.

Economic conditions, such as poverty or wealth, can significantly impact behavior. Limited resources and financial instability can lead to stress, anxiety, and a higher likelihood of engaging in risky or antisocial behaviors. Conversely, financial security can provide opportunities for personal growth and positive behaviors. The availability and accessibility of resources, such as education, healthcare, and recreational facilities, can shape behavior. For instance, limiting the child's knowledge base, or health care, limiting the child's physical well being, can restrict opportunities for personal development, affecting behavior patterns.

As educators, our personal beliefs provide a moral framework and a set of values to which we adhere. These values can shape behavior, decision-making, and interactions within the educational setting. We may emphasize concepts such as compassion, honesty, empathy, and respect for oneself and others. In many cases, this is attributed to our spiritual beliefs. Educators contribute to the environment by fostering a positive and ethical learning experience without imposing personal religious beliefs on students but recognizing that there is a connection that could be beneficial.

Integrating spiritual beliefs into the curriculum should be approached with sensitivity, respect for diversity, and an understanding of legal and ethical boundaries. Education systems must strive to create inclusive environments that respect the beliefs and values of all individuals while ensuring an unbiased and balanced approach to education. Incorporating spirituality into education can offer a greater sense of direction and significance. It can help students connect their learning experiences to something greater than themselves, such as a higher purpose, a divine plan, or a quest for personal growth. This sense of purpose can enhance motivation, engagement, and a deeper understanding of the subject matter.

The impact on the environment cannot be underestimated. For example, living in a noisy and chaotic environment can make concentrating difficult and increase stress levels. Conversely, a calm and peaceful environment can promote relaxation and well-being. Environmental factors such as air pollution and exposure to toxins can negatively affect physical and mental health, which can, in turn, impact behavior. It is essential to be mindful of the environmental factors that may be influencing our behavior and take steps to create a healthy and supportive environment whenever possible.

Teachers can design their classrooms in various ways to promote well-behaved and engaged students in learning. One key factor is the layout of the classroom. Teachers should arrange their classrooms in a way that maximizes space and ensures that students are not crowded. This will help students feel more comfortable and less restless. They may also use color to create a calming atmosphere in the classroom. Neutral colors like blue, green, and yellow are ideal for creating a peaceful environment.

Another way to design a classroom for good behavior is to give students a sense of ownership in the space. Teachers can do this by allowing students to decorate the classroom or giving them a say in arranging the furniture. This will help students feel more invested in the classroom and more likely to behave appropriately. Technology can be used to a teacher's advantage in designing a classroom; for example, teachers may use personalized learning tools or interactive whiteboards to engage students in the learning process. This will aid in maintaining student attention during instruction.

Teachers must establish clear rules and expectations for behavior in the classroom and follow them with consistency. This will help students understand what is expected of them and what behavior is appropriate. Teachers can also use positive reinforcement to encourage good behavior, such as giving out stickers or other rewards for appropriate behavior. Teachers can create a positive learning environment that benefits everyone involved by designing their classrooms to encourage positive behavior.

Lastly, the environment interacts with an individual's genetic makeup and inherent traits, leading to a unique combination of nature and nurture. While the environment plays a considerable role in shaping behavior, individuals also possess the capacity to make choices and adapt their behavior in response to various influences throughout their lives. The Bible states (KJV, 2017), "For sin shall not have dominion over you: for ye are not under the law, but under grace." With this, the development of personal resilience and support systems can mitigate some negative impacts of challenging environments and foster positive behavioral outcomes. The environment is a dynamic backdrop against which our beliefs manifest into behaviors. It provides the context, resources, and social cues that either reinforce or challenge our convictions, ultimately shaping how we engage with the world based on our beliefs.

THE IMPACT OF PHYSICAL DEVELOPMENT ON BEHAVIOR

Neuroscience research has demonstrated that various spiritual practices can activate different brain parts, providing long-term physical and mental benefits. Spirituality is a fundamental aspect of many people's lives and should be treated with respect and consideration (Amaral, 2021), as it is estimated that around 80% of people identify themselves as religious or practice spirituality-based rituals.

On the other hand, recent studies suggest that different brain regions mediate religious and spiritual experiences. These experiences can involve perception, cognition, and emotion. Importantly, there is increased activity in the frontal and prefrontal cortex during these experiences. The prefrontal cortex is responsible for executive functions, such as impulse control, decision-making, and goal-setting. Its development continues until early adulthood.

The Intersection Between Spirituality and Neuroscience (Cerqueira Rodrigues et al., 2023), suggests that practicing spirituality can cause changes in the parts of the brain that are responsible for chemical and biological reactions, leading to behavioral changes and a new perspective of the environment. Spiritual experiences can help individuals to better understand the world around them, resulting in improved discernment, empathy, and decision-making abilities.

According to Murakami and Campos (2012), religious practices can help individuals confront negative feelings such as anxiety and fear, and improve their mental health. Meditation, for example, has been shown to reduce tension, anxiety, and improve self-knowledge. Religion promotes values of cooperation and emotional well-being, and faith can produce beneficial emotions and improve the quality of life. "The practice of spirituality can alter parts of the brain related to chemical and biological reactions, resulting in behavioral changes and a new perspective of the environment. Spiritual experiences open the person up to the world, allowing for better discernment, empathy and better decisions (Cerqueira Rodrigues et al., 2023)".

Both genetic predispositions and environmental factors influence our ability to respond to outside stimuli appropriately. For example, a person with a genetic predisposition for anxiety may react differently to a stressor than someone without that predisposition. However, the individual's early experiences and upbringing can also shape how they respond to such stimuli. Science has proven making sound decisions matures over time, with the prefrontal cortex playing a crucial role in decision-making and impulse control. Adolescents are still developing this part of the brain and may not make sound decisions consistently as they develop into early adulthood.

According to Human Growth and Development (2022), these are the expectations at different stages of development: <u>Infancy</u> - There is a focus on meeting basic physical needs, such as nutrition, safety, and attachment. <u>Early Childhood</u> - The focus is on developing motor skills and language, as well as learning social norms and values, as expected. <u>Adolescence</u> - The focus shifts to cognitive development, moral reasoning becomes more complex, and adolescents are expected to take on greater responsibilities and make more independent decisions.

Physical development can affect behavior through its impact on self-esteem, body image, and overall physical health. For instance, an individual who develops a positive self-image and enjoys good physical health may be more confident in making life decisions. Furthermore, a nurturing environment and positive experiences during physical development can provide a strong foundation for developing self-control and the ability to make sound decisions. Much physical development is intertwined with behavior and decision-making throughout the human lifespan. Recognizing the intrinsic value of each punctuates the importance of promoting healthy development to enable individuals to make sound, moral, and ethical decisions. The process of making sound decisions matures over time, and it is essential to provide guidance and support at each stage of development to help individuals make informed and morally upright choices.

Chapter 3:

TRANSFORMING PERSPECTIVES: MINDSETS HAVE POWER

Our perception, whether negative or positive, influences our responses.

FRAMING EFFECT

Few educational challenges are as demanding as working with students facing behavior challenges, many of which can test your patience, creativity, and compassion daily. However, as educators, we are not alone in our quest to support these students. *The Joint Effect of Framing* (Giuliani et al., 2023), suggests that how we frame these challenges can significantly impact our effectiveness. Adopting a positive and empathetic mindset can create a more conducive learning environment for students.

The framing effect is a cognitive bias where the presentation of information about a student's behavior can influence decisions and perceptions. How information is presented can shape one's decisions, judgments, and behavior. Individuals react differently depending on whether the information is framed positively or negatively, even when the information is the Christiane. The framing effect demonstrates the power of perception and context in influencing choices and reactions. Understanding the framing effect is valuable, mainly when teachers are working with behaviorally challenged students. This understanding can help educators present information and situations in a manner that positively impacts behaviors in students that are both perplexing and demanding. Shifting our mindset when dealing with these challenges is vital and aligns with the spiritual traits of tolerance, commitment, and humility. These qualities should guide us as we begin to transform how we approach behavior issues in the classroom. I am reminded of a Bible scripture that informs my work with students, "Death and life are in the power of the tongue (Proverbs 18:21, KJV)". This scripture is meant to explain the power of our words. Educators should use words to uplift and inspire others, mirroring the positive framing effect.

Applying the framing effect from a spiritual context means looking at students not just for their past behavior but for their potential for growth and transformation. Teachers can frame their interactions with students to reflect grace and mercy, providing an opportunity for renewal and restoration. The research-based approach of restorative practices, rooted in forgiveness and redemption, can also positively impact behavior. Below are a few other viable options for encouraging appropriate behavior in students.

Framing Effect Examples -

1. *Positive Reinforcement* - Instead of saying, "Stop yelling out and being disruptive!" an educator might try, I appreciate how you are being attentive and respectful to your peers." Framing the feedback in this manner reinforces the desired behavior.

2. *Refocusing Attention* - instead of saying, "You're not paying attention", try to focus on a little-known fact and say, "Let's focus on this interesting topic we are discussing."

3. *Frame Expectations* - Instead of saying, Stop saying that in this classroom!" try, "In this class, we value kindness and

respect." This can set a positive tone and encourage students to meet the expectations.

4. *Self-Esteem Boost* - Instead of pointing out an area a student struggles in, try saying, "You're showing such improvement in your math word problems."

POWER OF MINDSETS

Our mindset refers to our fundamental beliefs, attitudes, and assumptions about ourselves and our environment. It is a mental framework that influences how we perceive and deal with challenges, success, and failure. Psychologist Carol Dweck (2012) popularized the concept of mindset and identified two primary types: fixed and growth mindsets. According to her research, "Students' mindsets can be affected by the subtle messages they receive from adults.' The role of a student's peers and their beliefs is significant as they can influence the student's mental framework through social contagion. While adults have a significant impact on a student's mindset, the more time they spend with peers, the more their peers' influence increases. This was suggested in the study, *Mindsets are Contagious* (King, 2020).

Studies have shown that people who believe their abilities and intelligence are fixed and cannot be changed may avoid challenges and give up quickly when faced with obstacles. This type of thinking can hold back personal and academic growth. Although having a fixed mindset can provide comfort and short-term success, it can also lead to difficulties in dealing with setbacks and negatively affect emotional well-being (Bedford, 2017).

On the other hand, having a growth mindset, which is the belief that abilities and intelligence can be developed through effort, learning, and perseverance, is more beneficial. Students with a growth mindset are more likely to take risks, welcome challenges, and view failure as a learning opportunity. They are better equipped to handle setbacks and promote their own personal and academic growth by seeking feedback and exhibiting resilience.

Mindset, whether fixed or growth, impacts an individual's

approach to challenges, learning, and success. While a fixed mindset may offer a sense of comfort, it can limit growth. In contrast, a growth mindset, emphasizing resilience and learning, aligns with the qualities of growth, stewardship, and humility. As educators, understanding these mindsets and fostering a growth-oriented approach can empower students to achieve their full potential (Nalipay et al., 2021). Parents and teachers seeking to help children develop should nurture their ability to embrace the growth mindset that begins prior to primary education.

Teachers who believe one's teaching ability can be improved have a growth mindset. On the other hand, those who believe that teaching ability is fixed have a fixed mindset (Nalipay et al., 2019). Those teachers who have a growth mindset are better able to model it, thus promoting it among their students. When teachers promote a growth mindset among students, it enhances their self-efficacy, task value, and self-regulation skills, which leads students to utilize skills such as accountability and self-discipline when facing emotional dysregulation (Bedford, 2017). Educators can create a positive change in the lives of their students by shifting their mindset towards growth and transformation. Applying that shift in the classroom can promote patience, kindness, forgiveness, and compassion, which is consistent with student growth.

Mindfulness training is an excellent resource for improving educational practices. While there are several beneficial approaches, mindfulness training helps educators to manage stress, regulate emotions, and become more self-aware, leading to a more patient and compassionate approach. Professional development programs focusing on behavior management, empathy, and understanding provide practical strategies and valuable insights. Mentoring and peer support programs offer platforms for sharing experiences and successful strategies. Culturally responsive teaching practices can also improve relationships with students from diverse backgrounds. Lastly, restorative practices, with their foundations in accountability, forgiveness, and redemption, have been shown to transform discipline and manage various behaviors effectively.

FRUSTRATION TOLERANCE

The role of teachers in education goes beyond imparting knowledge and skills; it involves modeling virtues that promote social and emotional well-being. Among these virtues, patience stands out as a critical skill that enhances communication and problem-solving and adds a sense of peace to the learning environment. Recent research emphasizes the importance of educators managing stress, setting realistic expectations, and utilizing effective conflict-resolution techniques to exhibit patient interactions with students. This modeling of appropriate behaviors creates an inclusive, supportive, and conducive learning environment.

The authors of *School Climate Factors Related to Teacher Burnout* (Grayson and Alvarez, 2008), emphasize the pivotal role of patience in education. They assert that patient teachers play a crucial role in facilitating student success. This patience allows educators to dedicate exceptional attention to each student, provide personalized feedback, allocate more time for instruction, and model patience for the students. These unilaterally enhance the student's overall comprehension and learning experience.

In addition to its practical benefits, patience has a spiritual dimension, as contemporary studies suggest. Mindfulness and meditation, often associated with spirituality, have contributed to greater self-awareness and emotion-regulating skills, which can be fundamental for cultivating patience in challenging situations. There is a growing need to consider spiritual practices in education to promote holistic development.

Research has highlighted the crucial role of teaching patience to students during their formative years. It equips them with a vital set of skills to navigate challenges that arise during their academic journey and beyond. To encompass the multifaceted nature of patience, educators can adopt a comprehensive approach. This approach can comprise mindfulness activities, problem-solving exercises, and thoughtful discussions about the significance of patience in diverse life situations.

Mindfulness activities are at the core of developing patience in students. They form the basis of cultivating self-awareness, encouraging students to adopt a calm and measured approach to problem-solving, and developing emotional regulation and resilience. Meditation, deep-breathing exercises, and reflective practices are some examples of mindfulness activities that can be employed to achieve these goals.

Ultimately, addressing issues related to impatience is critical in maintaining a harmonious and productive educational environment. When students learn to manage their impatience effectively, they are better equipped to face academic challenges, build stronger relationships, and adapt to the demands of an ever-changing world. Teaching patience is an investment in the future well-being and success of students, both in their educational journey and beyond.

The ability to tolerate frustration is essential in comprehending how to cultivate resilience, which is crucial for raising self-reliant and confident children. Research by Moss and Moses (2018) emphasizes that children can develop frustration tolerance as a learned skill rather than an innate trait. Parents, caregivers, and educators can actively shape a child's ability to manage frustration and obstacles. Identifying the triggers and signs of frustration allows us to intervene effectively and guide children toward healthier emotional responses. The authors also note various causes of frustration and how children express this frustration through different behaviors. This is why adults modeling patience, resilience, and practical problem-solving is vital to changing behaviors. Adults can lead by example to encourage children to emulate these qualities in their own lives. Equipping children with the ability to approach and solve problems systematically empowers them to tackle challenges more efficiently. Embracing a growth mindset will encourage students to view challenges as opportunities for growth.

THE MINDSET MODEL

The MindSet approach is based on four core principles: promote choice and trust, avoid power struggles, seek pro-action vs. re-action, and set-up everyone for success. The MindSet methodology (Purpose & Principle, 2023), aims to prevent problems by identifying and addressing potential risks. This proactive approach encourages individuals to cultivate a mindset that helps them recognize barriers, assess their vulnerability, and take appropriate action. From a spiritual context, mindset training may involve aligning one's thoughts and perspectives with your spiritual principles. It could encompass integrating faith-based beliefs into mindset techniques, such as relying on a higher power's strength, seeking wisdom from Scripture, and trusting in God's plan amid life's challenges. For example, someone dealing with anxiety might focus on scriptures about peace and trust in a higher power. Then, taking action means applying these teachings to daily life, by applying them during times of crisis. MindSet training involves reshaping thinking patterns to promote emotional and spiritual well-being.

This MindSet method serves as a crisis intervention; when in crisis individuals have the capacity to opt for non-aggressive responses if provided with the chance. Aggressive behavior often stems from fear and a feeling of powerlessness. However, fostering trust and offering opportunities for choice can effectively counteract these emotions. When individuals feel trusted and empowered to make decisions, it diminishes fear and the sense of powerlessness, consequently reducing the likelihood of resorting to aggressive behavior.

Next, we should maintain a supportive stance as an ally and be mindful of body language, prioritizing staying in your CAR (Calm, Aware, and Respectful) throughout the emotion. Handling a crisis effectively relies on appropriate timing, clear and balanced judgment without reacting too little or too much. When we develop these proactive strategies it will help in creating an environment conducive to learning. MindSet also emphasizes consistency and teamwork to help individuals thrive and effectively problem solve. MindSet training, whether secular or within a spiritual framework, aims to shape attitudes and beliefs to foster personal development, resilience, and a positive outlook on life.

Chapter 4:

CULTIVATING COMPASSION THROUGH SPIRITUAL PRACTICES

Cultivating compassion and understanding is the cornerstone of transformative education.

When we cultivate compassion for students through spiritual practices, we are simply self-reflecting, recalling past situations and experiences that bear a resemblance to the current one, and reflecting on how we would have preferred them to be handled. In educational settings, the integration of reflective practices emerges as a potent method for nurturing a compassionate and encouraging environment. Spiritual practices play a pivotal role in cultivating empathy, fostering understanding, and fostering a sense of interconnectedness among all individuals within the school community. However, both reflective and spiritual practices can overlap in certain contexts. By embracing these practices, conflicts can be minimized, and a heightened sense of self-efficacy can be promoted among staff, students, and families. While spiritual practices can be a form of reflective practice, not all reflective practices are spiritual. Reflective practices can encompass a wide range of activities, such as journaling, contemplation, and dialogue, that aim to deepen understanding and promote personal or professional growth without necessarily having a spiritual or religious foundation.

The practice of prayer is an integral part of the faith for many large religious groups, including Christianity, Judaism, Buddhism, and Islam. With approximately 2.6 billion followers, Christianity is the largest religion in the world, and prayer has a central role in Christian worship and spiritual practice. Similarly, Islam has 1.8 billion followers and strongly emphasizes prayer to connect with Allah and seek guidance and support. Regardless of religion, they recognize the power of prayer to provide comfort, inspiration, and a sense of connection to a higher power and encourage their followers to make prayer a regular part of their daily lives.

Prayer and meditation can be helpful spiritual practices for students in the classroom (Goralnik et al., 2020). They can provide a sense of peace and comfort and allow students to connect with something greater than themselves. Prayer can also help students develop a sense of gratitude and appreciation for the good things in their lives, which can improve their overall well-being and happiness. Additionally, prayer can be a way for students to express their hopes and desires for the future and to seek guidance and support as they navigate their educational journeys. Ultimately, prayer can be a powerful tool for spiritual growth and development and help students feel more connected to themselves, their classmates, and the world around them.

According to *Learning Worship* (Hidayah et al., 2021), the authors believe incorporating worship into the educational framework will improve student discipline, motivation, and academic performance. Worship practices encompass various spiritual and cultural traditions, promoting values including respect, self-discipline, empathy, and gratitude. This research suggests that when students engage in worship, they experience enhanced self-control, increased motivation, improved focus, and a sense of belonging within the school community. These positive outcomes ultimately contribute to improved academic achievements, creating a conducive learning environment for students. By recognizing worship as an essential aspect of student growth, schools can potentially optimize educational outcomes and nurture well-rounded individuals.

Many spiritual practices can be used to teach students to be self-aware. One effective approach is supporting them to engage in mindfulness meditation, which involves focusing their attention on the present moment and observing their thoughts and emotions without judgment. Another method used to foster gratitude among students is to prompt them to contemplate the good things in their lives and demonstrate gratitude for them. Additionally, practices such as coloring or journaling can benefit students' spiritual growth and development. The most important thing is to create a safe and supportive environment where students feel comfortable exploring their spirituality and developing a deeper understanding of themselves and their place in the world.

The Bible supports cultivating compassion. One of the most well-known passages is James 2:13, which states, "For judgment is without mercy to one who has shown no mercy. Mercy triumphs over judgment." This verse reminds us that we should be quick to show compassion to others, even if we feel they don't deserve it. Another scripture that supports cultivating compassion is Colossians 3:12, which encourages us to "clothe ourselves with compassion, kindness, humility, gentleness, and patience." This verse reminds us that compassion is not just a feeling but an action we can take daily (KJV, 2017).

Teachers and students who engage in spiritual practices have a heightened sensitivity that can help them respond with compassion and understanding. They may also incorporate contemplative practices such as journaling, self-reflection, or group discussions to explore and deepen their understanding the use of compassion. By reflecting on their own experiences, challenges, and emotions, teachers and students can gain insights into varying perspectives and develop a compassionate response.

A recent study examined the effects of another important practice, service learning, on youth development (Pong, Lam, 2023). Engaging students in service learning projects can foster compassion by providing them with opportunities to help others. Service learning activities, like volunteering in the community, can deepen students' understanding of social issues and encourage empathy and compassion toward those in need. The study highlights the positive impact of service-learning experiences on emotional intelligence, emphasizing their role in equipping participants with the capacity to comprehend and regulate their emotions proficiently. Beyond emotional intelligence, these experiences contribute to the cultivation of an adversity quotient, encompassing qualities such as resilience, adept problem-solving skills, and the capability to surmount obstacles. In essence, the study suggests that engagement in service-learning not only enhances emotional intelligence but also fosters a robust set of skills essential for navigating challenges and adversities effectively.

In *The Effects of Service Learning* (Pong, Lam, 2023), the results indicate that service-learning programs can significantly impact youths' emotional and psychological well-being, equipping them with valuable life skills. By actively engaging in community service, young individuals gain a broader perspective of the world and develop the necessary qualities to navigate challenges and thrive in adverse situations. Additionally, it highlights the importance of integrating service learning into educational curricula to foster holistic development among students, including processing emotions and overcoming adversity. As a result of its implementation, educators and policymakers can empower students to become socially responsible, resilient, and compassionate members of society. Increased classroom compassion and empathy lead to a more supportive and harmonious community.

Research also demonstrates that gratitude has a direct positive impact on a school's well-being. Students who practice gratitude experience higher levels of happiness, life satisfaction, and positive emotions, contributing to an overall sense of well-being within the school environment (Caleon et al., 2019). The research findings indicate that gratitude is crucial in positively influencing various aspects of school life. Gratitude serves as a catalyst, initiating a sequence of effects that impact interpersonal relationships, school resilience, and overall well-being. Gratitude enhances interpersonal relationships among students, fostering a positive and supportive social environment within schools. Grateful people tend to exhibit greater empathy, kindness, and prosocial behaviors toward their peers, creating a harmonious and inclusive school community. Furthermore, gratitude is found to contribute to the development of school resilience. Students who express gratitude are more likely to have higher levels of perseverance, adaptability, and coping skills. This resilience helps students navigate challenges and setbacks effectively, promoting a positive learning experience (Caleon et al., 2019).

Creating a positive and nurturing learning environment is essential as a teacher, and cultivating compassion is a vital aspect of achieving this. One way to achieve this is by incorporating spiritual practices into your daily routine. You can better understand your students' needs and perspectives by reflecting on your values and beliefs. This will help you approach teaching with empathy and compassion, which can create a safe and supportive space for your students to learn and grow. To enrich your spiritual practice, take a few moments each day for self-reflection as you contemplate your thoughts and emotions. Develop a sense of gratitude and appreciation for the blessings in your life, which can help to shift your focus from what is lacking to what is achievable. By making these practices a regular part of your routine, you can become a more effective and compassionate teacher and help your students academically and emotionally thrive.

One way of cultivating compassion in the classroom is by encouraging students to put themselves in each other's shoes. By asking students to consider how they would feel in another person's situation, they can develop empathy and understanding for their peers. Teaching mindfulness and meditation can help students become more aware of their own emotions and those of others, leading to a more compassionate and empathetic classroom environment. Modeling compassion and kindness as a teacher can significantly impact students and reinforce the importance of these values in the classroom.

Chapter 5:

MINDFULNESS AND ITS CONNECTION TO BEHAVIOR

Engaging in spiritual practices helps us develop a mindful connection with ourselves and our destiny.

The link between mindfulness and behavior becomes evident through an increased level of self-awareness. Mindfulness enables us to identify recurring behavioral patterns, such as automatic reactions or impulsive responses. By gaining awareness of these patterns, we can interrupt them and opt for more deliberate and beneficial behaviors. Mindfulness plays a crucial role in behavior by fostering self-awareness, emotional regulation, stress reduction, improved decision-making, and enhanced relationships. Through mindfulness practice, we can develop a more robust command over our behavior and learn to respond to situations more intentionally. Regular engagement with mindfulness contributes to positive individual and social outcomes.

Regarding student behavior, mindfulness can meaningfully influence how students perceive and respond to their thoughts and emotions. In a study, *"Listen to the Children,"* researchers conducted interviews with the participating students of an elementary school. The study included various mindfulness exercises and activities designed to enhance self-awareness, attention, and emotional regulation (D'Alessandro et al., 2022).

In the opinion of D'Alessandro (2022), students had positive perceptions of the mindfulness intervention. Many expressed enjoyment and engagement in the mindfulness activities, finding them helpful in managing stress, improving focus, and regulating their emotions. The students reported feeling calmer and more relaxed after practicing mindfulness techniques. Additionally, the students added how practical and transferable mindfulness skills are in everyday life. They noted applying mindfulness techniques during challenging situations, such as tests or peer conflicts, to stay calm and make better choices. The students valued the opportunity to learn and practice mindfulness at school, recognizing its potential benefits for their overall health.

Interestingly, the study highlighted the critical nature of considering students' perspectives when implementing school mindfulness programs. The idea emphasizes that elementary school children can understand and appreciate mindfulness practices, finding them valuable for their emotional and cognitive development. The research supports the integration of mindfulness interventions in educational settings to support children's mental health and well-being (D'Alessandro et al., 2022).

In today's society, the youth are having difficulty with emotional regulation. According to research (Martin & Ochsner, 2016), the study illuminates how understanding the brain processes involved in regulation of emotions can inform educational practices and interventions. Moreover, our emotional regulation skills develop over time and are influenced by brain maturation and environmental factors. The brain regions undergo considerable developmental changes throughout childhood and adolescence. Understanding these neural processes can provide insights into children's challenges in regulating their emotions and inform the design of educational strategies to promote effective emotion regulation. The article also suggests that educators can have a crucial role in supporting the development of these skills through targeted interventions. Through mindfulness practice, we can expand our skill of non-reactivity to the students' emotions. It enables us to observe our emotions without being overwhelmed or immediately acting upon them. This allows for teachers to develop greater emotional self-regulation and to enhance their ability to respond to situations more thoughtfully and effectively.

Mindfulness helps both teachers and students avoid unwanted behaviors that may be driven by intense emotions, allowing for more measured and constructive responses. This consistent practice can lead to less stress and being more likely to exhibit calm and composed behavior rather than being overwhelmed by stress-induced reactions. Ultimately, less stress enhances our decision-making ability. We can make more deliberate and informed choices, consider various perspectives, weigh consequences, and be aware of our biases that may trigger our emotional regulation. Mindfulness strategies allow us to make decisions that align with our values and long-term goals, leading to more positive and adaptive behavior.

As described in *The Neuroscience of Emotion Regulation* (Martin & Ochsner, 2016), educators need to create supportive environments that foster the skills for emotional regulation. The article suggests incorporating mindfulness practices, social-emotional learning programs, and explicit instruction on emotional regulation techniques into the curriculum. By promoting the development of emotional regulation skills, educators can enhance students' academic performance as well as social interactions. Researchers believe there is potential to translate neuroscience research into practical strategies that can be implemented in educational settings. By bridging the gap between research and practice, educators can provide effective interventions to support students' emotional regulation development, eventually improving their educational outcomes and emotional well-being.

DEVELOPING CONSCIOUS AWARENESS THROUGH SPIRITUAL PRACTICES

Self-awareness lays the foundation for personal growth. It empowers students to make conscious choices aligned with their values rather than acting on automatic or unconscious patterns. Spiritual practices also enhance students' emotional intelligence and self-regulation. By learning techniques such as mindfulness and meditation, students gain the ability to observe their thoughts and emotions without judgment, leading to greater emotional resilience and improved mental health. These practices provide valuable tools for managing stress, anxiety, and other challenges students may face. In addition to personal growth, spiritual practices will make way for more empathy, compassion, and understanding toward others. They encourage students to develop a sense of interconnectedness and foster a culture of respect and acceptance within the educational setting. Spiritual practices promote a positive, inclusive educational environment. Students can express themselves and connect meaningfully. Developing conscious awareness through spiritual practices in education acknowledges the holistic nature of human beings. Education that focuses solely on intellectual development neglects the emotional, social, and spiritual dimensions of students' lives. By integrating spiritual practices into education, schools recognize the importance of nurturing the whole person and supporting students as a whole.

Developing conscious awareness through spiritual practice in the classroom with sensitivity can be challenging yet rewarding for teachers. Teachers can begin by fostering an environment of mindfulness and empathy, where students feel comfortable sharing their thoughts and emotions freely without worrying about being judged or criticized. Teachers can lead by example, practicing meditation or other spiritual practices and sharing their experiences with their students. By doing so, teachers can help their students develop a deeper understanding of themselves and others while cultivating compassion and connection.

Additionally, incorporating themes of spirituality into lesson plans and classroom discussions can help students broaden their perspectives and develop a more nuanced understanding of the world around them. In the end, the key to developing conscious awareness through spiritual practice in the classroom is to broach the topic with sensitivity and respect, recognizing that each student may have their own unique beliefs and experiences.

Chapter 6:

MINDFULNESS-BASED BEHAVIOR MODIFICATION TECHNIQUES

Behavior modification, rooted in faith, transforms you, while behavior manipulation yields only temporary results.

Behavior modification in students refers to systematically applying techniques and strategies to promote positive behavior and discourage negative behavior in an educational setting. It involves modifying the environment, implementing specific interventions, and reinforcing desired behaviors to facilitate learning and create a classroom environment conducive to learning. Behavior modification in students typically focuses on identifying and addressing behaviors that may disrupt learning, impede social interactions, or hinder academic progress. The goal is to replace undesirable behaviors with more appropriate and constructive ones.

Behavior modification in students is focused on creating a positive and supportive learning environment, promoting self-regulation, and helping students develop appropriate social and academic skills. By employing evidence-based techniques and individualizing interventions, behavior modification strategies can effectively support students in achieving their educational and behavioral goals.

Developing mindfulness-based behavior modification techniques is essential because they combine the principles of mindfulness with behavior modification strategies to help students make positive changes in their thoughts, emotions, and behaviors. As I noted, these techniques can be effective in countless areas of life. One example of a proven technique is mindful breathing, which involves focusing one's attention on the breath and observing the inhalation and exhalation without judgment. It helps students cultivate awareness of the present moment and can be used to calm the mind, reduce stress, and promote relaxation.

In the study, *The Effectiveness of Daily Mindful Breathing Practices* (2016), students who participated in daily mindful breathing exercises reported significant reductions in test anxiety levels. Mindful breathing, as a form of mindfulness practice, helped students cultivate greater awareness of their thoughts and emotions, allowing them to approach test situations more calmly and in a more focused way. The findings underscore the potential of incorporating mindfulness techniques into educational settings as a valuable tool for enhancing students' emotional well-being and academic performance (Cho et al., 2016).

Another technique discussed in educational research is *body scan meditation,* which can be an excellent tool for teachers to use in their classrooms. By guiding their students through a simple meditation exercise, teachers can help them become more focused and present. Teachers can ask their students to sit comfortably with their eyes closed. They can then guide them through a series of steps, starting with focusing on their breath and then gradually moving their attention to different parts of their body. As students scan their bodies, they can become more aware of any tension or discomfort they may be experiencing. By acknowledging these sensations without judgment, they can learn to release them and become more relaxed and centered.

The authors of *Consciousness and Cognition* (2012) show how body-scan meditation was found to enhance somatosensory perceptual decision-making. This involves making judgments based on sensory information from the body, like touch and temperature. Those who practiced body-scan meditation exhibited improved decision-making compared to a control group. This highlights the positive impact of even brief mindfulness practices on tactile information processing, which can be beneficial for students dealing with anxiety or stress. It is a simple yet effective technique that teachers can incorporate into daily routines to foster focus, presence, and self-awareness in the classroom, creating a more supportive learning environment (Mirams, L. et al., 2012).

Another technique that has proven successful in shaping and modifying behavior is called self-monitoring, and it simply involves observing and recording one's own behavior and its antecedents and consequences. In this mindfulness-based approach, individuals can bring mindful awareness to their behaviors, noticing patterns, triggers, and the impact those behaviors have on their thoughts and emotions. By mindfully monitoring their behavior, individuals can gain insights into the underlying factors contributing to their actions and make more conscious choices.

Self-monitoring can help students develop better behavior in the classroom. By encouraging students to keep track of their own behavior and progress, teachers can help them to become more aware of their actions and work towards positive change. Teachers should establish clear objectives and collaborate with students to create explicit behavioral goals. Classroom goals may include following rules, meeting deadlines, and showing respect. By setting clear goals, students will better understand what is expected of them.

Teachers can provide students with tools for self-monitoring, such as checklists or behavior charts, which will help students to track and monitor their behavior as well as progress toward their goals. The Behavior Queen (www. behaviorqueen.com) believes that if we "Rule Less, Teach More" and provides excellent resources in this area. Teachers should encourage reflection. This could involve asking students to write about their experiences or setting aside time to discuss their progress with them. Finally, teachers should provide regular feedback about their student's behavior and progress. This could involve praising students for positive behavior or providing constructive feedback for areas that need improvement. By working with their students to set clear goals, providing tools for self-monitoring, encouraging reflection, and providing regular feedback, teachers can help their students to become more aware of their actions and work towards positive behavior change.

Another resource for teachers is *Acceptance and Commitment Therapy* (ACT) (Hayes et al., 2016). ACT is a mindfulness-based approach that emphasizes accepting uncomfortable thoughts, emotions, and sensations while committing to behaviors aligned with one's values. It encourages individuals to observe their experiences mindfully without trying to change or suppress them. By mindfully accepting their present experience, individuals can choose behaviors that align with their values and make positive life changes.

One resource introduces readers to ACT as a type of psychotherapy that blends mindfulness and behavioral techniques to foster psychological flexibility and promote meaningful, value-driven behavior. The book explores the six core processes of ACT: acceptance, cognitive defusion, being present in the moment, self-as-context, values clarification, and committed action. It provides practical guidance on how to apply these processes to various psychological and emotional challenges, such as anxiety, depression, chronic pain, and relationship issues. This approach can help teachers and other educators to work with their students to understand how to develop psychological flexibility by learning to accept complex thoughts and emotions, defuse unhelpful cognitive patterns, and engage in actions aligned with their values and goals. ACT may also be used in conjunction with the previously discussed mindfulness behavior modifications.

Cognitive defusion is rooted in acceptance and commitment therapy; it involves creating distance from thoughts to observe them without feeling overwhelmed. In children, this approach helps to manage intense emotions. Utilizing preventive techniques like mindfulness exercises, storytelling, and open communication help cultivate the process of cognitive defusion. By teaching these skills, we empower children to navigate their emotions more effectively, fostering healthier behavior.

One way to incorporate Acceptance and Commitment Therapy (ACT) in your classroom to help your students develop a positive mindset, cope with stress, and build resilience is to encourage your students to practice mindfulness exercises, such as deep breathing and body scans, before starting a task or during a break. This can help them focus on the present moment and reduce anxiety about the future or regrets about the past. Another way to use ACT is to help your students identify their values and set meaningful goals aligning with them. This can help them stay motivated and feel purposeful in their studies. Finally, you can model ACT principles by using positive self-talk and reframing negative thoughts, which can encourage your students to do the Christiane. By incorporating ACT into your teaching, you can help your students develop the skills they need to succeed academically and emotionally.

Another effective method for improving student behavior in the classroom is through *stimulus control*. This involves altering the environment in which the behavior occurs to increase the likelihood of the desired behavior and decrease the likelihood of undesirable behavior. In this mindfulness-based approach, individuals can practice being aware of their environment and the triggers that lead to certain behaviors. By mindfully noticing these triggers, individuals can make conscious choices and respond more intentionally and in a more controlled manner.

To implement stimulus control, teachers should identify the specific behaviors they want to see more or less of. Then, they can adjust the classroom environment to encourage the desired behaviors and discourage the undesirable ones. For example, if a teacher wants students to focus more during class, they can remove distractions such as unnecessary clutter or bright, distracting decorations. They can also rearrange the seating so students face forward and away from potential distractions. Alternatively, if teachers want to encourage participation and engagement, they can add visual aids, provide hands-on activities, and incorporate group work into the lesson plans. Teachers can create an environment that supports positive student behavior and learning outcomes by incorporating stimulus control techniques in the classroom.

Yest another resource for teachers is explained in the book *Retrain Your Brain* (2020). This examines Cognitive-Behavioral Therapy (CBT), a well-established therapeutic approach focusing on how thoughts, emotions, and behaviors are interconnected and influence one another. The book provides readers with practical tools and exercises to identify and challenge negative thought patterns, helping them understand how their thoughts can affect their emotions and behaviors. Using CBT techniques, teachers can learn to help students retrain their brains and develop healthier thought patterns, leading to more positive emotional responses and constructive behaviors.

Another area that CBT emphasizes is the importance of recognizing cognitive distortions, such as negative self-talk, catastrophizing, and all-or-nothing thinking. Through guidance, students can replace harmful thought patterns with more balanced and realistic thoughts. Taking control of their mental and emotional health by applying CBT principles to retrain their brains and foster lasting positive change can reduce anxiety, depression, and other negative emotional states, improving their overall mental health (Firpo-Cappiello, 2020).

As a teacher, you can use cognitive restructuring in your classroom to help your students overcome negative thinking patterns and develop a more positive outlook. For example, if a student says, "I'm bad at math," you can ask them to reframe that thought by saying, "I'm still learning math, but I can improve with practice." This can help students develop a growth mindset and feel more empowered to tackle challenging tasks. Additionally, you can model positive self-talk and encourage your students to do the Christiane. By cultivating a classroom culture of positivity and resilience, you can help your students develop the skills they need to succeed academically and personally.

Mindfulness-based behavior modification techniques are not just reserved for students. Any of these techniques can be used with teachers and students in classrooms by incorporating daily practices into the curriculum. This can include brief mindfulness exercises at the beginning and end of each class and longer mindfulness sessions during specific parts of the day. These practices can help students and teachers to become more aware of their thoughts, feelings, and actions and to regulate their behavior more positively and productively.

Teachers can use any or all of these mindfulness techniques to model effective and compassionate communication, which can help to improve relationships among students and between students and teachers. By integrating mindfulness-based behavior modification techniques into the classroom, teachers and students can develop greater self-awareness, emotional intelligence, and overall well-being. These examples illustrate how mindfulness-based behavior modification techniques can be applied in various domains of life, offering individuals practical tools to cultivate their abilities to manage stress and improve emotional regulation for meaningful behavioral changes.

Chapter 7:

Integrating Ethical Considerations into Behavioral Management

Social-emotional learning is like a compass that guides us beyond academics, teaching us to navigate our emotions.

Bringing Ethics into the Classroom (2014) argues for including ethics education in the academic setting. It highlights three essential components, frameworks, multiple perspectives, and narrative sharing; as effective methods to facilitate ethical learning. The first area is the framework: the research believes that ethical frameworks are the basis for teaching ethics in the classroom. These frameworks provide students with structured approaches to analyze and address ethical dilemmas. By understanding various ethical theories and principles, students can develop a systematic way to assess and resolve moral issues they may encounter. Behavior is one aspect that is a challenge in many educational environments. Frameworks can become an actionable item to help shape students' behaviors positively.

One effective framework is the "Four Way Test," which asks students to consider whether their actions are truthful, fair, beneficial, and respectful. Another approach is to use Case Studies and Role-playing Exercises to help students practice making ethical decisions in real-world situations. By using frameworks like these, teachers can empower students to develop critical thinking skills and ethical reasoning abilities that will serve them well throughout their lives. Providing students with different ethical frameworks, teachers can help students develop a broader understanding of ethical reasoning and decision-making.

These frameworks then allow students to analyze ethical issues from multiple perspectives and develop their own ethical frameworks for making moral choices. The authors argue that incorporating these frameworks into ethics education can help students navigate complex ethical challenges more effectively in their personal and professional lives. When we view multiple perspectives or help students explore them freely, it may help shape and guide them using ethical reasoning. When students explore various viewpoints, they begin to appreciate the complexity of ethical decisions and the cultural, social, and personal factors that influence their lives. Exposure to diverse opinions fosters open-mindedness and empathy, allowing students to make more informed and balanced ethical judgments (Marthur and Corey, 2014).

Finally, therapeutic storytelling and narrative sharing are also powerful tools to engage students in ethical decision-making. Real-life stories and personal experiences provide concrete examples of ethical challenges and their consequences, making the subject matter more relatable and meaningful. Students can learn from these narratives, enhancing their ethical awareness and critical thinking skills. By incorporating frameworks, multiple perspectives, and narrative sharing, educators can create a comprehensive ethics education that equips students with the knowledge, empathy, and abilities to navigate ethical dilemmas responsibly and honestly.

Integrating ethical considerations into behavioral management in the classroom aids is an important component of creating a safe and objective learning environment for students. One way to achieve this is by setting clear expectations and rules that promote respect, responsibility, and accountability. Establishing consequences that are reasonable and consistent with the behavior in question is a critical piece of this process. Teachers should also consider each student's individual needs and backgrounds and strive to create a sense of community and inclusivity in the classroom. By integrating ethical considerations into behavioral management, teachers can help students develop the skills and values necessary to succeed in school, community, and life. Consistency and clear expectations will communicate expectations to students. If we discuss implementing ethical principles, the expectations should be grounded in ethics, such as treating others with kindness and respect, taking responsibility for one's actions, and showing empathy towards peers. We can introduce ethical values explicitly in classroom discussions and lessons. We can discuss concepts like honesty, integrity, fairness, and compassion, and explore real-life scenarios that require ethical decision-making.

Educators may also consider modeling ethical behavior by demonstrating this behavior in their actions and interactions with students and colleagues. Students are more likely to emulate ethical behavior when they witness it in their teachers. Modeling promotes critical thinking and ethical reasoning by encouraging students to consider the consequences of their actions on themselves and others. Encouraging discussions where students can explore ethical dilemmas and make well-informed decisions is the final important set in this process.

Holistic Approach to Behavior Management

By implementing positive reinforcements, we fulfill the wisdom of Proverbs 22:6: 'Train up a child in the way he should go, and when he is old, he will not depart from it.' We must acknowledge and commend students for displaying ethical behavior and making morally responsible decisions. This encourages them to continue acting in ethical ways. Emphasize restorative practices rather than punitive measures when addressing behavioral issues. These practices focus on repairing harm and rebuilding relationships, fostering empathy and accountability. Additionally, encourage students to develop empathy by helping them understand and consider the feelings and perspectives of others. This can lead to more compassionate and understanding interactions within the classroom.

To build a strong classroom community, you may start by taking inspiration from Romans 12:5, which reminds us that we are one body in Christ, with each individual being a member of the other. Encourage collaborative activities and teamwork to create an environment that fosters mutual support. Regularly reflect on ethical challenges and invite students to journal or discuss their moral growth and actions. This will help nurture self-awareness and character development. With this holistic approach, we can create a positive and supportive learning space that benefits students and teachers alike.

Another means of creating lasting change that shapes behavior is to include Social-Emotional Learning (SEL) Programs in daily interactions. *Implementing Social-Emotional Learning in the Elementary Classroom* (2023) notes that the COVID-19 pandemic dramatically changed the way teachers delivered instruction, reminding us of the importance of "Maslow before Bloom" (Raschdorf et al., 2020). The phrase "Maslow before Bloom" implies a priority in education, suggesting that fulfilling the basic needs and psychological well-being of students, as emphasized by Maslow's hierarchy of needs, should come before focusing on higher-level cognitive skills and educational objectives, as advocated by Bloom's Taxonomy.

Students' social-emotional needs should be met before expecting them to absorb and retain academic information. The benefit of social-emotional lessons is that they explicitly teach students about relationship skills, emotions, empathy, and responsible decision-making. When SEL is used purposefully and faithfully, it helps students develop the emotional intelligence needed for ethical behavior and improve relationship skills. Delving into SEL programs will allow you to gain valuable insights into fostering a positive and inclusive classroom and school culture, to address disciplinary issues with fairness and empathy, and to implement proactive strategies to promote student well-being and success.

SEL lessons aid in emotional regulation, fostering empathy, and promoting responsible decision-making, thereby helping students to exhibit improved self-control and better behavior. SEL also nurtures empathy, enabling students to build positive relationships, reduce conflicts, and navigate social situations more sensitively. Moreover, it encourages critical thinking, leading to responsible decision-making, fewer impulsive choices, and enhanced communication skills. SEL further addresses issues like bullying, promotes academic achievement, reduces stress, boosts self-esteem, and imparts valuable life skills. We are reminded in Proverbs 4:23, 'Above all else, guard your heart, for everything you do flows from it.' This underscores that Social and Emotional Learning (SEL) is a powerful tool that can foster a positive school climate, creating an environment where students are more likely to exhibit desirable behavior and thrive academically and personally. Learning the critical nature of various intervention programs and approaches to support students with diverse learning needs and behavior challenges will be central to your role in ensuring that all students have access to quality education and nurturing adults who are passionate about the whole child and their mental and spiritual development.

Chapter 8:

BEHAVIOR MODIFICATION TECHNIQUES

Behavior modification is the pursuit of long term behavior change through the use of evidence-based strategies, while behavior manipulation influences behavior only temporarily.

The NAEYC (National Association of Educators of Young Children) Position Statement shared that there are far more children with special needs (including those with disabilities, those at risk for disabilities, and those with challenging behaviors) participating in typical early childhood settings today than in the past (NAEYC, 2020). It follows then that our nation needs help developing and maintaining a qualified teaching force to tackle increasing educational behavior challenges. To avoid teacher "burnout," veteran and novice teachers must embrace their ability to channel inner peace, proven behavior modification techniques, and to accept the idea that this profession serves a greater purpose, one embedded in spiritual awareness.

Spirituality can play a significant role in behavior modification by tapping into an individual's deeper values and beliefs and providing a powerful motivational framework for positive change. By aligning behavior modification goals with spiritual principles, students can draw upon their sense of purpose and connection to foster lasting transformation. For example, affirmations and visualizations have become very popular to motivate oneself. These can reinforce the desired behavior by creating a sacred space for personal growth and reaffirming a person's commitment to change. This approach not only enhances the efficacy of behavior modification but also promotes a sense of inner harmony and fulfillment by integrating spiritual values into daily actions. Tapping into our spirituality introduces the concept of self-transcendence and a connection to something greater than oneself.

This broader perspective can motivate students and teachers alike to move beyond immediate gratification and consider the impact of their actions on others and the world at large. By fostering virtues like compassion, patience, and self-discipline found in many spiritual teachings, they can navigate challenges with resilience and remain dedicated to their behavior modification goals. Ultimately, spirituality offers a profound framework that intertwines personal growth, ethical conduct, and a sense of purpose, enriching the behavior modification process with a deeper and more sustainable dimension of change.

Behavior modification techniques are fundamental tools in special education and can have an important impact on the learning and development of students with diverse needs and behavioral issues. Over the years, various techniques have been researched and applied to address challenging behaviors in education but are not limited to special education students, as many general education students have significant behavior issues as well. One well-established behavior modification technique is Positive Behavior Support (PBS). PBS is a comprehensive approach focusing on preventing and addressing challenging behaviors by creating a positive and supportive environment. Research consistently shows that PBS effectively reduces problem behaviors and improves social skills among students with disabilities (Horner et al., 2005). By identifying the underlying causes of challenging behaviors and implementing individualized interventions, PBS promotes positive outcomes for all students.

Another technique is Applied Behavior Analysis (ABA), a widely used behavior modification technique for students with Autism Spectrum Disorders (ASD). ABA involves breaking down complex behaviors into smaller, manageable components and using reinforcement strategies to encourage desired behaviors while reducing challenging ones. Numerous studies have demonstrated the effectiveness of ABA in improving communication and social skills, and reducing problem behaviors in children with ASD (Smith et al., 2000). ABA's structured approach allows for data-driven decision-making, ensuring interventions are tailored to individual needs.

Cognitive-behavioral interventions (CBI) represent a technique that addresses behaviors by targeting thought patterns and emotions. CBI is often used with students experiencing anxiety, depression, or conduct disorders. Research indicates that CBI can improve emotional regulation and reduce students' tendency to internalize their problems (Kendall et al., 2011). By teaching students strategies to identify and challenge negative thought patterns, CBI empowers them to develop healthier coping mechanisms.

Functional Communication Training (FCT) is specifically designed to address communication-related challenging behaviors, such as aggression or self-injury. FCT focuses on teaching students alternative, more appropriate ways to express their needs and desires. Studies show that FCT can significantly reduce problem behaviors by providing individuals with a means to communicate effectively (Tiger et al., 2008). This approach recognizes the importance of communication as a fundamental skill.

Finally, Peer-mediated interventions involve training peers to support and facilitate positive behaviors in students with disabilities. Research has consistently demonstrated the benefits of peer-mediated interventions, including increased social interactions, improved academic engagement, and reduced problem behaviors (Carter et al., 2014). These interventions not only benefit the students with disabilities but also contribute to a more inclusive and supportive classroom environment.

Behavior modification techniques are diverse and versatile, offering individuals a range of strategies to address challenging behaviors in students with disabilities. Research plays a large role in guiding the selection and implementation of these techniques, highlighting their effectiveness in promoting positive outcomes. The choice of technique should be based on a thorough understanding of the student's needs and characteristics, ensuring that interventions are tailored to their unique circumstances.

Chapter 9:

Effective Communication and Active Listening

The difference between communication and effective communication is the people actively listening.

Effective communication in schools and in life carries a profound spiritual dimension. It emphasizes the practice of mindful presence, a core principle in many spiritual traditions. It starts with educators and students being fully present in their interactions, fostering a deep and meaningful connection. This mindful presence enhances understanding and aligns with the idea that each moment holds significance within the spiritual journey.

Spirituality also encourages empathy and compassion, which are expressed in effective communication. When individuals genuinely listen to others, acknowledge their emotions, and respond with kindness and understanding, they tap into their spiritual potential. This compassionate communication enriches relationships and reflects the essence of many spiritual teachings.

From a spiritual perspective, all beings are interconnected. Effective communication recognizes this interconnectedness, underscoring that the well-being of one influences the well-being of all. Thus, fostering harmonious relationships through communication aligns seamlessly with spiritual principles that emphasize the unity of all life. When we examine active listening as a spiritual practice, it involves moments of silent reflection, creating space for contemplation and self-awareness. This practice encourages deep listening in the school environment and provides opportunities for personal spiritual growth through reflection.

Empathetic understanding is another core spiritual value that is nurtured through the practice of active listening. By actively listening, individuals open themselves to truly understand the perspectives and experiences of others, fostering unity and compassion in line with spiritual ideals. Spirituality often places great value on diversity and the enrichment it brings to life. Active listening in schools acknowledges and celebrates the diversity of voices, opinions, and experiences. It fosters an inclusive and spiritually enriching environment that appreciates the unique contributions of every person. Schools play a pivotal role in imparting moral and ethical values to students. Effective communication, when infused with spiritual principles, becomes a means to convey values such as compassion, forgiveness, tolerance, and respect for others. We can build a sense of community rooted in principles of openness and mutual respect, fostering a sense of belonging and interconnectedness within the school community.

When behavior is viewed through a spiritual lens, effective communication and active listening in schools become potent tools for nurturing the skills as mentioned earlier among students, educators, and the larger school community. These skills enhance the educational experience and contribute significantly to individuals' spiritual growth and well-being. By fostering harmonious relationships, resolving conflicts peacefully, and embracing diversity, schools can create an environment that aligns seamlessly with spiritual principles and values, ultimately promoting a more holistic and spiritually enriching educational journey.

Listening effectively is key to addressing behavior challenges in individuals, as proven by extensive research in education, which consistently shows that active and empathetic listening is essential in understanding the underlying causes of the behavior challenges. Active listening allows educators to identify triggers, environmental factors, or emotional issues contributing to the behaviors, which is needed for developing targeted and effective interventions. Also, studies reveal that students with behavior challenges are more likely to respond positively to educators who actively listen, as this approach conveys genuine interest and builds trust and rapport over time. Effective listening provides educators with insights into each student's unique needs and experiences, which helps in customizing interventions. It also improves communication skills, not only for educators but also for students with behavior challenges, leading to more constructive interactions. Active listening can de-escalate conflicts, prevent behavior challenges from escalating, and improve students' emotional regulation. It fosters inclusive and supportive classroom environments where students feel heard, respected, and valued, ultimately promoting positive behavior outcomes and a conducive learning atmosphere. Therefore, active and empathetic listening remains a fundamental component of successful behavior management strategies in educational settings.

To practice active listening, you must give your full attention to the speaker by eliminating distractions and maintaining eye contact. Nonverbal cues, like nodding and maintaining an open posture, demonstrate your engagement and encourage the speaker to express themselves more freely. Be careful not to interrupt the speaker as it can disrupt the flow of conversation and make the speaker feel unheard. Instead, allow the speaker to finish before responding. Verbal affirmations, such as saying "I understand" or "That makes sense," signal that you are following the conversation. Reflecting and paraphrasing what the speaker has said can help ensure understanding and show that you are actively processing the information. Asking clarifying questions when needed and using empathetic and validating language can foster a supportive atmosphere. Active listening also requires patience, as some speakers may need more time to express themselves. Reserving judgment, practicing self-reflection, and remaining open to different perspectives and experiences is essential. By incorporating these strategies, individuals can become more skilled active listeners, improving their relationships and understanding in both personal and professional contexts.

Chapter 10:

UNDERSTANDING AND DEALING WITH CHALLENGING BEHAVIORS

Just as every student is unique, so are the approaches we must embrace to manage behavior, tailored to their strengths and unique needs.

Having a thorough understanding of challenging student behaviors is absolutely critical, as these behaviors have a direct and significant impact on the quality of education that is provided. The behaviors can disrupt the learning process, hindering the affected student and their peers from achieving their full academic potential. The behaviors often emerge due to past trauma, neurological, environmental, and psychological influences. Identifying and addressing these behaviors is a priority for creating a conducive learning environment. Educators can prevent behavior issues from escalating by understanding their nature and causes and providing early intervention and support. Challenging behaviors often indicate underlying mental health or emotional issues, making identifying and addressing them essential to support students' well-being.

Educators can provide tailored interventions to create a fair and inclusive learning environment by understanding each student's behavior. Addressing challenging behaviors is also critical for maintaining a safe school environment, as some behaviors, like aggression or bullying, can pose significant safety risks. Furthermore, it equips students with essential life skills such as emotional regulation, conflict resolution, and communication, which are invaluable for their future success. Finally, involving parents and guardians in addressing these behaviors through understanding is often vital to effective intervention, as a collaborative effort between home and school can be more effective in supporting the student.

In sum, understanding challenging behaviors in students is integral to their academic success, mental and emotional well-being, and long-term personal development. Challenging student behaviors have been a longstanding concern for educators, parents, and society. These behaviors encompass a wide range of actions that disrupt the learning environment, hinder academic progress, and affect the overall well-being of students and their peers.

While various factors contribute to the development and persistence of challenging behaviors, I want to focus on the potential role of spirituality in influencing the outcomes. Spirituality, which we know is often intertwined with religion, involves a deep connection to something greater than oneself and can provide a person with a sense of purpose, meaning, and moral guidance. By examining the relationship between spirituality and challenging behaviors in students, we can shed light on how spiritual beliefs and practices contribute to better understanding, managing, and ultimately transforming these behaviors.

Challenging behaviors can manifest as aggression, defiance, withdrawal, inattention, and other disruptive actions which are defined below. Understanding the root causes and characteristics of these behaviors should take precedence for educators, counselors, and researchers seeking effective strategies for addressing them. "The Ministry of Education in Toronto, Canada states that challenging behaviors can include but are not limited to:

- Aggression: physical or verbal acts of aggression towards others.

- Defiance: open resistance or refusal to follow rules or instructions.

- Withdrawal: social isolation, disengagement, or avoidance of peers and activities.

- Inattention: difficulty focusing, following directions, or completing tasks.

- Disruptive behavior: actions that disrupt the learning environment and hinder the educational process"

Addressing challenging student behaviors requires a nuanced and holistic approach that recognizes the potential influence of spirituality while considering individual differences, cultural diversity, and ethical considerations. Acknowledging and respecting students' spiritual beliefs and practices can create an inclusive and supportive educational environment, promoting personal growth, resilience, and positive behavior outcomes. Continued research will further deepen our understanding of this intricate relationship, paving the way for more effective interventions and support systems in the educational setting.

Dealing with Aggression and Defiance

Once we have an understanding of the students' needs, we must gradually begin to shift our thinking as we address the behavior. Taking a spiritual perspective means staying calm and compassionate when faced with aggression and defiance. The first step is finding inner peace and clarity during the conflict, drawing strength from one's spiritual beliefs. Understanding the root causes of such behavior and practicing empathy is essential. Often, aggression and defiance stem from fear, insecurity, or unmet needs. It is important to actively listen, forgive, and communicate nonviolently to bridge the gap between individuals. Mindfulness and meditation help us stay grounded, while prayer and affirmations maintain hope and connection to our spiritual values. Setting boundaries with kindness, seeking support from spiritual communities, and modeling these values in our behavior all contribute to a more peaceful and spiritually aligned approach to handling aggression and defiance. We can promote personal growth and well-being for all involved with patience and persistence.

Dealing with aggression and defiance in students requires a thoughtful and multifaceted approach that prioritizes the student's well-being while maintaining a safe and conducive learning environment. As you shift your intentions, consider these strategies:

Remain Calm and Maintain Self-Control: Remain calm and composed. Avoid escalating the situation by reacting emotionally and engaging in a power struggle. Model the behavior you want to see in your students.

Ensure Safety: Prioritize the safety of all students and staff. If a student's behavior becomes physically aggressive, take immediate steps to remove other students from harm's way.

Build Positive Relationships: "You must connect before you correct!" (Clay, 2010). Establishing positive, trusting relationships with students is paramount. Students are more likely to cooperate and engage positively with adults if they have a connection rooted in trust and respect.

Set Clear Expectations: Communicate clear and consistent behavior expectations in the classroom. Ensure students understand the rules, consequences, and rewards for their actions and apply these consistently.

Offer Choices: Provide students with choices within reasonable boundaries. This can give them a sense of control and reduce defiance. For example, you might offer choices related to assignments or activities. During de-escalation, you can take a walk or a break in the calming area of the room.

Use Positive Reinforcement: Acknowledge and reward positive behavior. Positive reinforcement can be highly effective in motivating students to exhibit desired behaviors. During de-escalation, practice praising minimal compliance.

Teach Self-Regulation Skills: Help students develop self-regulation skills, such as emotional awareness and coping strategies. Provide guidance in managing frustration, anger, or other challenging emotions, e.g., deep breaths, refocusing on task, setting short-term goals.

Implement Behavior Plans: Develop individualized behavior intervention plans (BIPs) for students who frequently exhibit aggression or defiance. BIPs outline specific strategies and interventions to address challenging behaviors, e.g., speaking to a preferred staff member, high-quality attention, reduced downtime, planned breaks.

Provide a Safe Space for Expression: Empower students and allow them to express their feelings or concerns in a safe and non-confrontational way. Sometimes, defiance can be a result of underlying emotional issues.

Use De-escalation Techniques: Learn and apply de-escalation techniques to defuse tense situations. These may include active listening, offering choices, and using a calm and non-confrontational tone.

Involve Parents and Guardians: Keep the lines of communication open with parents or guardians. Collaborate with them to develop strategies for managing behavior at home and school.

Seek Professional Help: If a student's aggression or defiance persists and significantly disrupts the learning environment, consider involving school counselors, psychologists, or behavior specialists who can conduct assessments and provide targeted support.

Teach Conflict Resolution: Incorporate conflict resolution and problem-solving skills into the curriculum. Encourage students to work through disagreements constructively.

Restorative Practices: Implement restorative justice practices that focus on repairing harm, building empathy, and fostering accountability among students, e.g., classroom norms/agreements, community circles.

Continuous Professional Development: Stay informed about classroom management and behavior intervention best practices. Be a lifelong learner, and enhance your skills with workshops and training.

Remember that addressing aggression and defiance in students is an ongoing process. You must be patient, consistent, and committed to understanding the underlying causes of these behaviors. Continuous professional development and a commitment to understanding each student's unique needs and triggers will be invaluable during this process. Flexibility and adaptability in your approach help students develop positive behaviors and attitudes over time.

Chapter 11:

INTEGRATING EMOTIONAL REGULATION TECHNIQUES

Emotional regulation can be achieved when we balance both negative and positive feelings.

Educators, caregivers, and professionals can enhance their ability to address challenging behaviors while supporting emotional development by integrating evidence-based emotional regulation methods into behavior management plans. Behavior management fosters positive social and emotional growth across age groups. However, it is now recognized that addressing emotional dysregulation in some individuals requires more than traditional behavior management approaches.

Emotional regulation involves recognizing, understanding, and effectively managing emotions, which are vital for navigating relationships and social situations. Poor emotional regulation often leads to challenging behaviors like aggression and withdrawal, making it a critical focus for behavior management. Incorporating mindfulness into daily routines is essential for improving emotional well-being. As previously noted, practices like deep breathing and meditation enhance self-awareness, promoting balance and calmness. Integrating mindfulness into behavior management can encourage emotional self-regulation.

Emotion coaching validates and guides individuals through their emotional experiences and helps them label and manage emotions, reducing emotional outbursts. Cognitive-behavioral therapy identifies and changes negative thought patterns that cause emotional instability, making it a practical component of behavior management plans to target challenging behaviors' root causes.

Several studies indicate that using emotional regulation techniques improves the effectiveness of behavior management. For instance, Jones et al. (2018) found that students receiving emotion regulation training reduced aggressive behaviors. Similarly, Smith and Johnson (2019) demonstrated that emotion coaching strategies effectively reduced defiance in children with behavioral challenges. The practical application involves implementing emotional regulation techniques in various settings. Introducing mindfulness exercises into daily school routines helps students manage stress and improve behavior.

Integrating emotional regulation into behavior management is a promising approach to address challenging behaviors while promoting emotional well-being. By recognizing the importance of emotional regulation and applying evidence-based strategies, individuals and professionals can create more effective behavior management plans supporting positive outcomes and emotional development. Integrating emotion regulation techniques into behavior management can enhance the overall quality of life and success for those struggling with emotional dysregulation.

Encouraging students to identify and label their emotions helps them communicate their feelings more effectively. Simple but effective breathing exercises like square breathing can swiftly calm heightened emotions. Positive self-talk and problem-solving skills empower students to challenge negative thoughts and address the root causes of their emotions. Using stress balls and other tangible items can be beneficial for managing behavior as they provide a physical outlet for negative emotions and energy. When we feel stressed or anxious, our bodies often respond with tension and restlessness. Using a stress ball or other physical object to release this tension can help calm our minds and reduce our stress levels. Having a tangible item to focus on can distract us from negative thoughts or behaviors, allowing us to regulate our emotions and reactions better. Implementing behavior management strategies, such as labeling emotions, positive self talk and stress balls, can be a practical and effective way to improve emotional well-being.

Another option for regulating is to have an emotional regulation journal. It equips students with a tangible resource for managing their feelings. We can better understand our emotional patterns and triggers by regularly recording our thoughts, feelings, and behaviors. This increased self-awareness can help us identify and address negative thought patterns or behaviors which contribute to stress or anxiety. Having a designated space for writing enables them to articulate, express, and navigate their emotions. This, in turn, can offer a sense of release and relief, contributing to a heightened feeling of being grounded and centered in their daily lives. An emotional regulation journal can be a valuable resource for adults and students looking to improve their emotional regulation and overall mental health.

Students thrive and are successful in a structured and predictable classroom environment, which provides a sense of safety and emotional security. Predictability is crucial for emotional regulation, fostering stability, and reducing anxiety. Knowing what to expect from their surroundings and daily routine helps students feel more in control, boosting their self-esteem and confidence. A predictable classroom environment promotes a positive learning community by fostering connections between peers and teachers. Creating a predictable classroom environment is essential for promoting emotional regulation and facilitating a conducive learning environment for students and reduces the opportunity for emotional dysregulation.

A recent study into *"the effects of a structured classroom"*

(Glenna et al., 2020) investigates the impact of implementing a structured classroom management system in high school resource classrooms, specifically for students with special needs. The study presents five essential elements of classroom management, including positive expectations, specific praise, group contingency reinforcement, individual reinforcement, and responses to inappropriate behavior, which are introduced systematically to create a well-structured system. The article explores how this structured approach affects classroom behavior and academic engagement in secondary resource classrooms, offering practical strategies for managing classrooms with diverse student needs.

Unlike previous research that has examined individual components of classroom management separately, this study takes a different approach by introducing and integrating five key elements of classroom management in a step-by-step manner. The sequential introduction of these elements proceeds as follows: (a) establishing and teaching positively framed expectations, (b) implementing specific and contingent praise, (c) incorporating group contingency reinforcement systems, (d) integrating individual reinforcement systems, and (e) utilizing in-class responses to address inappropriate behavior.

Undoubtedly, integrating emotional regulation techniques in the classroom can be highly beneficial to the learning environment. Educators who use these skills to their students facilitate better decision-making, foster healthier relationships, and promote academic excellence. Emphasizing emotional regulation aids educators in creating a positive environment that directly contributes to student success. Prioritizing emotional regulation is critical in cultivating a successful student learning experience.

Chapter 12:

UNDERSTANDING THE SIGNIFICANCE OF TRAUMA

Dealing with trauma gives us the strength to mend and reshape the patterns of our future.

    Trauma is an experience that can leave deep scars on an individual's psyche, affecting their emotional, psychological, and even physical well-being. Trauma disrupts an individual's sense of safety and trust in the world, making it essential to understand its multifaceted nature. Educators need to recognize that students who have experienced trauma may exhibit a wide range of behaviors that can be challenging to understand without proper context. These behaviors can include withdrawal, aggression, inattentiveness, and emotional outbursts.

    Trauma can encompass many experiences, from physical and emotional abuse to loss, neglect, or exposure to violence. The consequences of trauma can persist long after the traumatic event has occurred, impacting a student's ability to engage in the classroom and hindering their overall development.

Research has shown that traumatic experiences during childhood, referred to as Adverse Childhood Experiences (ACEs), may have a long-lasting effect on a person's mental and emotional health. The Centers for Disease Control and Prevention (CDC) conducted a study and found that individuals with more ACEs were more likely to face health and social issues later in life, including substance abuse, depression, and even shorter life expectancy (Webster EM, 20222).

From a spiritual perspective, recognizing trauma aligns with the biblical mandate to show compassion and care for those who are suffering. Jesus emphasized the importance of empathy and care for the vulnerable and wounded. In the Good Christianaritan parable (Luke 10:25-37), Jesus illustrated the principle of helping those in need, even if they are strangers. In recognizing the signs of trauma in students, educators can follow Jesus's example by being attentive and compassionate. Doing so can create a safe and supportive environment where students feel understood and valued.

Trauma-informed teaching is an approach that acknowledges the impact of trauma on students' behavior and focuses on creating a nurturing and safe learning environment. Numerous studies have highlighted the benefits of trauma-informed practices in schools. For instance, a research study published in the Journal of Applied School Psychology (2018) found that implementing trauma-informed strategies led to a significant decrease in disruptive behaviors and an increase in students' emotional regulation.

Educators can utilize research-based strategies to recognize signs of trauma in students. These strategies include observing changes in behavior, listening actively to students, and seeking additional information from parents or guardians when necessary. By combining research findings with spiritual principles of compassion and understanding, educators can create a more empathetic and practical approach to recognizing and addressing trauma in the classroom. Recognizing trauma is the first step towards creating a classroom environment that fosters healing and growth.

To be trauma-informed educators, we must be vigilant in recognizing the signs of trauma (Honsinger & Brown, 2019) in our students. Some common indicators may include:

Changes in Behavior: Sudden shifts in behavior, such as increased aggression, withdrawal, or emotional volatility, can indicate underlying trauma.

Academic Struggles: Students who have experienced trauma may have difficulty concentrating, completing assignments, or participating in class.

Social Isolation: Trauma can lead to a sense of alienation, causing students to isolate and detach themselves from peers.

Physical Symptoms: Unexplained physical symptoms like headaches or stomach aches may also be signs of trauma, as the body's response to stress can manifest in physical ailments.

Regulating, Relating, Reasoning

Dr. Bruce Perry's Neurosequential Model of Therapeutics (NMT) is a well-known and influential approach for helping children whose brains have been affected by stress and trauma. NMT highlights the significance of addressing the unique requirements of the stressed brain in a specific order to achieve maximum results (Perry & Szalavitz, 2017). It outlines three crucial and sequential phases for evaluating and managing challenging behaviors in children, commonly referred to as the "3 R's". The concepts of regulating, relating, and reasoning can be used in conjunction with biblical scriptures to provide an individual with greater understanding.

When we regulate, we are establishing a sense of safety, both physically and emotionally, in order to manage behavior effectively. Perry's approach emphasizes that before we can help someone, particularly children, we must create an environment where they feel secure. The Bible supports this approach in Psalm 46:1, "God is our refuge and strength, an ever-present help in trouble" (KJV). This verse illustrates the concept of seeking refuge and safety, much like what we aim to provide in the regulation phase.

Relating involves building meaningful connections and relationships with individuals throughout the process. The model and the Bible both highlight the noteworthiness of empathy and compassion in human interactions. In Galatians 6:2, we find, "Carry each other's burdens, and in this way, you will fulfill the law of Christ" (KJV). This verse stresses the significance of relating to others by actively participating in their lives, listening and showing care, mirroring the concept of relating advocated by Dr. Perry.

Reasoning implies engaging in higher-level thinking, perspective-taking, reflection, and problem-solving. Dr. Perry and the Bible both acknowledge that practical reasoning is possible when trust and emotional stability are established. For instance, in Proverbs 2:6, "For the Lord gives wisdom; from his mouth comes knowledge and understanding" (KJV). This verse prioritizes wisdom and understanding as gifts from God, and they are more readily accessible when we are emotionally stable and receptive, much like the child who has been regulated and has established a trusting relationship with an adult.

By embodying the NMT approach, we can better understand the interconnectedness of psychology and spirituality in the context of behavior management. Redemption and transformation resonate with many religious beliefs, suggesting that even amid trauma, individuals can find strength and purpose through their faith. Prayer and meditation on scripture can offer comfort and direction. Seeking professional help, like therapy, should be seen as a complement to one's faith journey. Encouraging patience and trust in divine timing recognizes that healing from trauma is a gradual journey, where faith provides unwavering support and hope at each stage.

Chapter 13:

HEALING, RESTORATION, AND RESILIENCE

Spirituality fuels growth, enhances our understanding of behavior, and leaves a lasting impact on our interactions.

Once we recognize trauma in students and the importance of approaching their pain with empathy, we can draw upon spiritual understanding and practical techniques that may aid individuals in their healing journey. At its core, spirituality is faith centered on redemption, healing, and restoration. Religious texts are replete with stories of individuals who faced adversity, trauma, and brokenness but found healing and restoration through their faith in God. Importantly, these biblical narratives offer awareness of how we may address the healing and restoration of individuals who have experienced trauma.

From a spiritual perspective, faith and trust in God are foundational to healing and restoration. The Bible teaches us that placing our trust in God's plan can lead to transformation and renewal. In Proverbs 3:5-6, we find guidance: "Trust in the Lord with all your heart and lean not on your own understanding; in all your ways submit to him, and he will make your paths straight" (KJV). Educators can encourage students to trust in a brighter future despite their traumatic experiences. We can help them understand that their faith and the support of caring adults can be a source of strength and healing.

Forgiveness is a central theme in spirituality. Religious teachings emphasize the importance of forgiving others as an important path to personal healing and restoration. Matthew 6:14-15 states, "For if you forgive other people when they sin against you, your heavenly Father will also forgive you. But if you do not forgive others, your Father will not forgive your sins" (KJV). Educating individuals about the transformative power of forgiveness not only benefits the one being forgiven but also the forgiver. Encouraging students to let go of bitterness and anger can be a significant step toward healing.

In *Resilience in Mental Health* Rutten et. al. explain that being resilient is more than just not having a mental illness. It is an ongoing process that helps people handle difficult situations throughout their lives. In essence, taking steps to prevent or lessen the impact of challenges on your mental and physical health, and having the capacity to rebound quickly from any problems that arise . Accordingly, nurturing resilience in students who have experienced trauma is needed to help them heal and grow. Developing strength is essential as it enables us to recover from difficult situations (2013).

Community plays a pivotal role in fostering and developing resilience. Through community connections, individuals can access emotional and social support, which bolsters their ability to cope with adversity and stress. These connections offer a sense of belonging and reduce the feelings of isolation that often accompany challenging times. Christianity underscores the influence of community and fellowship. The church is often called the "Body of Christ," highlighting the idea of individuals being interconnected and meant to support one another. In Galatians 6:2, we read, "Carry each other's burdens, and in this way, you will fulfill the law of Christ" (KJV). Educators can foster a supportive classroom community by encouraging students to seek help from one another, mirroring

Christian principles of fellowship and care.

Trauma-Informed Teaching Strategies

Integrating trauma-informed teaching strategies in schools has become necessary in today's classrooms where many students are dealing with or have experienced trauma. These strategies are grounded in both research and empathy, aligning with spiritual values of gentleness and understanding. Research has demonstrated the efficacy of the following techniques in supporting those who have encountered this kind of damage.

Creating a Safe and Predictable Environment

Research has shown that a safe and predictable environment is central for students who have experienced trauma. A study published in the "Journal of Child and Adolescent Trauma" (2017) found that students in trauma-informed classrooms reported feeling safer and more supported. We can also implement strategies such as clear routines, consistent rules, and a calm classroom atmosphere to capitalize on their feeling of safety.

Building Positive Teacher-Student Relationships

Strong teacher-student relationships are at the heart of trauma-informed teaching. This concept aligns with the religious principles of providing refuge and security for those in need. According to research published in the "Journal of School Psychology" (Bunting, 2020), positive teacher-student relationships can mitigate the effects of trauma on students' behavior and academic performance. Extending grace, empathy, and unconditional positive regard toward students will maximize the feeling of interconnectedness. When we demonstrate care and understanding, we create a foundation for healing and growth.

Trauma-Sensitive Classroom Practices

Trauma-informed teaching focuses on implementing practices that consider the needs of students who have gone through traumatic experiences. This encompasses understanding triggers and providing alternatives to punitive discipline. A study published in the "National Library of Medicine" (2019) found that trauma-sensitive approaches reduced disciplinary incidents and improved students' emotional regulation. Applying practices like restorative justice, mindfulness, and sensory interventions are options. These approaches recognize that punitive measures can potentially cause further harm and hinder the healing process. Therefore, utilizing approaches that prioritize healing can benefit their overall well-being.

Chapter 14:

RECOGNIZING AND RESPECTING CULTURAL DIFFERENCES

Celebrating cultural differences helps to promote self-awareness and a better understanding of the world around us.

Being self-aware of cultural differences helps us recognize and overcome biases. Acknowledging that different cultures may have unique communication styles, values, and social norms is appropriate. A study by Matsumoto and Juang (2017) highlights the complexities of intercultural communication and stresses the significance of recognizing these nuances to prevent misunderstandings and promote productive communication.

Despite the reality that our world continues to have serious cultural divisions, in the midst of these ongoing problems, our country has become increasingly diverse. A new world has emerged with diversity within schools, churches, and communities. Many religious texts urge us to "live at peace with everyone," emphasizing the critical nature of harmony and respect in our interactions. This concept aligns with the qualities of empathy and understanding, which highlight the need to recognize and adapt to cultural differences.

Respecting cultural differences extends to religious practices and beliefs, with a growing body of research exploring interfaith dialogue and understanding. Recent works like those by Abu-Nimer and Nelson (2021) emphasize the importance of religious literacy and respect for diverse faith traditions. This research revealed that more than 80% of the world's population adheres to faith, and the theory of diversity, peace, justice, forgiveness, and reconciliation are aspects of all religions. The question is not "If" a person participates in religious acts but "How." The conversation is no longer exclusive to churches, institutions, or faith-based organizations. It is being discussed in schools, board rooms, and within policies (Abu-Nimer and Nelson, 2021).

We are charged with understanding the significance of religious freedom and the need to respect and learn from other faith traditions. The Torah encourages believers to "Love your neighbor as yourself" (The Torah, 1962/2015, Leviticus 19:18), emphasizing the importance of showing love and respect to all individuals, regardless of their faith background. Acknowledging and respecting the variations in communication styles, values, traditions, and religion fosters a sound atmosphere that allows for mutual learning among students, adults, and all stakeholders while promoting inclusivity and respect.

Cultural Sensitivity in Behavior Management

According to a study conducted by Linda Darling-Hammond and colleagues in the field of education in 2023, teachers may unknowingly possess biases and stereotypes that affect their disciplinary actions. To counteract this, it is essential to adopt practices such as self-reflection and awareness, as advised in *Long-term Reduction in Implicit Race Bias* (Devine et al., 2012).

Devine and colleagues' explored research on reducing implicit bias in 2012. The study in question evaluates the efficacy of interventions designed to break prejudicial habits. It went further to examine the effectiveness of interventions intended to reduce implicit biases in individuals, particularly race-related ones. The interventions involved fostering awareness and strategies to counteract tendencies. The study found that mindfulness was a successful intervention that helped an individual focus on the present moment rather than other thoughts that serve as a distraction. Another intervention the researchers discussed was Individuation, where participants were encouraged to focus on the uniqueness of individuals rather than relying on broad stereotypes. This is similar to another intervention called Perspective-Taking, where participants were encouraged to consider situations from the perspective of individuals from different racial backgrounds to guide the exercise. The above-mentioned interventions helped to foster empathy and understanding. Regularly using these and other strategies will aid educators in remaining vigilant against making unfair judgments based on cultural factors.

Cultural sensitivity is a foundational principle for effective teaching, especially in diverse classrooms. Educators who recognize and respect cultural differences create an inclusive learning environment that empowers students to feel valued and confident in their learning. Cultural competence will enable us to understand and address cultural factors that should inform our practices when working with diverse populations.

The concept of cultural sensitivity is broad; however, we should consider different cultural norms, such as eye contact and body language, when discussing behavior management. For example, in some cultures, direct eye contact could be seen as a sign of disrespect; in others, it is considered a sign of attentiveness. Educators should be aware of these nuances and avoid misinterpreting a student's behavior based on their cultural background. Consider including classroom discussions about cultural differences in communication styles within classroom activities, encouraging students to share their experiences and learn from each other.

Creating a culturally sensitive classroom involves respecting and valuing students of all cultural backgrounds. Teachers may utilize literature and stories from various cultures to expose students to diverse perspectives, helping them appreciate different worldviews. When we purposefully include students' cultural experiences in the curriculum, we make learning more relatable and engaging. Building strong partnerships with parents and guardians is also a powerful strategy for effective behavior management. You could include families and the community in the learning process by hosting multicultural events, workshops, and training. When we collaborate with parents and community members from diverse backgrounds, it not only enhances the educational experience but also demonstrates respect for students' cultural contexts.

Addressing Bias and Stereotypes in Behavioral Management

Failing to address biases and stereotypes within the classroom will inadvertently impact best practices. It should be the goal of the educator to ensure equity when establishing a behavioral management system in the classroom. Since cultural biases and stereotypes are ingrained beliefs and assumptions about individuals or groups based on their cultural and ethnic backgrounds, they may be subtle and go unnoticed. However, they may manifest in our interactions, decision-making process, and behavior management strategies for particular students. Denying the existence of implicit biases will only hinder personal growth and classroom progress.

It would be beneficial for all educators to participate in cultural competence training. This training will help participants understand and gain knowledge about different cultures, including their values, customs, and communication styles. The process will require self-awareness and adaptability. A helpful technique to utilize in the classroom is Counter-Stereotypic Imaging. It challenges stereotypes by having students imagine scenarios that go against stereotypes, which may ultimately change their ingrained perceptions For example, a career day where role models have succeeded in a field typically associated with a certain stereotype. Educators may assign a research project requiring students to explore the accomplishments or contributions of individuals from different cultural backgrounds. Addressing the issue head-on will promote cultural sensitivity and encourage fair and unbiased judgments.

Chapter 15:

THE ROLE OF FUNCTIONAL BEHAVIOR ASSESSMENTS

Every action we take, every gesture we make, and every expression we display, serves as a means of communication.

Functional Behavioral Assessment (FBA) (Romani et al., 2023) is a critical tool for anyone who works with students with problem behaviors. The primary purpose of an FBA is to uncover the root causes and triggers behind a student's challenging behavior. The approach involves examining the function of each behavior: attention, escape, access to tangibles, and sensory stimulation. By examining the antecedents, behaviors, and consequences, FBAs provide valuable insights into why certain behaviors occur. This comprehensive analysis helps us formulate effective behavior intervention plans (BIPs) tailored to each student's unique needs.

Many people believe that Functional Behavior Assessments are exclusively for students with disabilities. However, while it was initially developed for special education students, recent research has proven its effectiveness in the general education setting (Filter & Alvarez, 2012). We can effectively tackle socially unacceptable behavior by identifying the target behaviors that need to be reduced and the antecedent that triggers them.

In the early 1990s, the research on FBAs was centered around two students who showed similar behaviors, but the function of their behavior was different. This led researchers to emphasize the importance of identifying the unique function of each behavior (Filter & Alvarez, 2012). Over time, the focus shifted towards replacing unwanted behaviors with more appropriate ones using positive interventions instead of negative consequences.

FBAs have consistently proved to be effective in various educational settings. When done thoroughly, this approach helps educators understand the driving factors behind problem behaviors. This understanding then allows us to design more effective and targeted interventions. By implementing evidence-based strategies identified through FBA, we often see significant improvements in student behavior.

FBAs go beyond addressing the surface-level symptoms of behavioral issues; they aim to change behavior at its core. We can promote positive student behavior changes by identifying the underlying causes and employing proactive strategies. While the extent of these changes may vary from case to case, the ultimate goal is to replace undesirable behaviors with more appropriate ones, improving students' well-being and ability to thrive academically and socially.

Additionally, it is vital to determine the appropriate interventions for each grade level based on the challenging behaviors exhibited by students. For instance, in elementary school, interventions maybe designed to increase attention and on-task behavior. In middle school, interventions may focus on reducing disruptive behaviors and improving self-regulation. High school students might need interventions to address emotional regulation and anxiety. College students may benefit from interventions that enhance time management and goal-setting skills to improve academic performance. In order to address problematic behaviors effectively and implement appropriate interventions tailored to each student's specific needs, it is crucial to conduct a comprehensive Functional Behavioral Assessment (FBA). This will ensure a holistic approach to behavior management and help identify the underlying causes of the behaviors in question.

The following information is Adapted from the National Center on Intensive Intervention (2013) Handout 3c: A-B-C *Report Form,* part of *Using FBA for Diagnostic Assessment in Behavior.*

In order to support students with diverse needs and learning styles, educators should implement various strategies that can adjust the difficulty of tasks, enhance engagement, and foster a positive learning environment. Some approaches for dealing with behaviors that are negatively reinforced through the escape or avoidance of tasks:

Adjust the Difficulty of the Task:
- Offer easier work to ensure students can successfully complete the task.
- Decrease the amount of work to prevent overwhelming the students.

Offer Choice:
- Allow students to choose:
    - Which task to complete.
    - The sequence of tasks to be completed.
    - Which materials to use.
    - Where to complete the task.
    - When to complete the task.
    - With whom to complete the task.

Increase Student Preference/Interest in the Activity:

- Incorporate student hobbies and interests into activities.

Assure that Activities are Functional or Relevant for the Student:

- Provide a rationale for school tasks or activities that is meaningful in the student's everyday life or related to their future goals.
- Use functional tasks to teach or practice academic skills.

Alter the Length of the Task:

- Shorten the activity to keep students engaged.
- Provide frequent breaks to prevent fatigue.

Modify the Mode of Task Completion:

- Allow students to choose between response methods (e.g., oral, written, typed) that suit their preferences and abilities.

Use Behavioral Momentum and Task Dispersal:

- Present easy requests before difficult ones to build momentum and motivation.

Increase Predictability:

- Provide cues for upcoming activities or changes in activities, whether instructional, visual, or auditory. For example, use a 5-minute warning or maintain a regularly reviewed picture schedule.

Modify Instructional Delivery:

- Reduce the complexity of language used in instructions.
- Adjust the rate of speech to ensure comprehension.

- Check students orally for understanding.
- Use a pleasant tone of voice to create a positive learning environment.
- Present instruction in the student's preferred modality to enhance understanding and engagement (e.g., using visual aids or hands-on activities).

By incorporating these strategies, educators can better meet the diverse needs of their students and create a more inclusive and effective learning environment.

Behavior Intervention Plan

According to *A Practical Guide to Writing Behavior Intervention Plans* (Higgins et al., 2023), Individuals with Disabilities Education Act (IDEA) suggests creating a Behavior Intervention Plan (BIP) guided by the Functional Behavior Assessment (FBA) when a child's actions hinder their own or other students' learning. A Behavior Intervention Plan (BIP) is a personalized strategy designed to support students who exhibit challenging behaviors that interfere with their learning or that of others in the classroom. Its primary purpose is to systematically address and modify these behaviors by implementing targeted interventions. The BIP aims to identify the root causes or triggers of the challenging behavior through assessments like Functional Behavior Assessments (FBAs). By understanding the function or purpose behind the behavior, the plan can then outline specific strategies, supports, and techniques to proactively address these behaviors. It is essential that BIPs be individualized, have clear outlining, have strategies tailored to the student's unique needs, and contain measurable goals.

The authors (Higgins et al., 2023), collectively identified the following 11 components of a "quality BIP":

1. Introductory section

2. Target behavior

3. Hypothesized function and statement(s)

4. Goals

5. Antecedents

6. Antecedent interventions

7. Replacement behaviors

8. Interventions to be taught

9. Consequences

10. Consequence interventions

11. Data collection methods

The goal of implementing a Behavior Intervention Plan is not just to manage challenging behaviors reactively but to equip students with alternative, more appropriate behaviors while fostering a positive learning environment. Successful measurable outcomes of a BIP include a reduction in the frequency or intensity of the challenging behavior, improved social and emotional skills, enhanced participation in classroom activities, and overall academic progress, ultimately promoting a supportive and conducive learning environment for the student and their peers.

Chapter 16:

Applying Behavioral Management in Real-Life Scenarios

Employing intimidation to address negative behavior represents a short-term remedy for a long-term challenge.

Daryl's Disruption -

Daryl is a fourth-grade general education student, and teachers are growing concerned about his behavior. He is exhibiting disruptive behavior in the classroom. During direct instruction, Daryl frequently interrupts the lesson, distracts his peers, and struggles to use self-control.

When students' social, emotional, or sensory needs are unmet, they may exhibit attention-seeking behavior, such as disruptions and distractions. We are charged with supporting Daryl's growth and development, and we recognize that patience and guidance are paramount to effectively managing his behavior. As noted throughout, religious texts encourage us to be patient and understanding as we train children.

One viable method for addressing Daryl's disruptive behavior is the implementation of Positive Behavioral Interventions and Supports (PBIS) (See Chapter 8). The majority of your students will respond to this behavioral system. Although, for Daryl, a teacher might consider making adjustments to meet his individual behavioral needs. With PBIS, teachers set clear expectations, students receive positive reinforcements for desired behaviors, and the method provides corrective feedback when needed. Essentially, PBIS offers a structured framework to foster positive behavior and create a conducive learning environment for most students in the classroom.

Vickii's Academic Struggles

Vickii is a seventh-grade student who is struggling academically. Her difficulty accessing the curriculum leads to frustration and disruptive outbursts in the classroom. Vickii's behavior affects students' learning and creates tension in the classroom environment.

Vickii's behavior could result from her lack of access, so she misbehaves to escape doing the work or to hide from peers that she does not understand what is being asked of her. Educators should recognize and nurture each student's unique gifts and potential, promoting a positive and inclusive learning environment.

Implementing a personalized learning approach will allow Vickii to process at her own pace and explore the concept in a way that she finds comfortable. The teacher should tailor lessons to the students' needs and interests, giving them autonomy and engagement. Personalized learning always involves core elements - targeted instruction that is flexible and intentional, data-driven decisions with assignments that are purposeful, self-reflection and ownership.

Kelli's Dilemma

Kelli, a sixteen-year-old high school student, has faced academic challenges, including grade retention, and is currently enrolled in the tenth grade while retaking ninth-grade classes from the previous school year. He receives support in a small group setting as a special education student. Kelli's difficulties extend beyond academics, as he grapples with peer conflicts and exhibits aggression towards both staff and peers. These behaviors have resulted in disciplinary consequences and emotional distress.

Kelli has an Individual Education Plan (IEP) with a Behavior Intervention Plan to manage his behaviors. In addition to implementing the IEP with fidelity, the teachers should encourage Kelli to embrace empathy and reconciliation as a means to resolve conflicts and foster a compassionate school community. This will create an inclusive and supportive learning environment where Kelli can thrive academically and personally.

The adoption of restorative practices represents a research-based approach with a focus on repairing harm and rebuilding relationships. Recent research conducted by Lodi et al. (2022), underscores the effectiveness of restorative practices in reducing suspensions and enhancing the overall school climate. An example of this approach includes conducting restorative circles and conferences to address conflicts, which would allow Kelli to express his feelings, gain insight into the impact of his actions, and collaborate towards a resolution. By applying these strategies, educators can provide Kelli with the necessary support to navigate his challenges and create a positive and supportive learning environment.

Oriana's Trauma

Oriana, a 5th-grade student, has experienced severe trauma, including losing a parent and witnessing domestic violence. These damaging events have left her struggling with challenging behaviors, including angry outbursts, withdrawal, and difficulty forming healthy relationships with peers and authority figures.

The religious texts encourage us to "Love our neighbor as ourself." As a starting point, we approach Oriana with compassion and empathy, recognizing her pain and loss. We provide her a safe space to express her feelings and fears, fostering trust and openness.

We incorporate trauma-informed strategies, recognizing the impact of past experiences on Oriana's behavior. This approach helps us provide support and healing for her emotional wounds. Next, we introduce mindfulness and self-regulation techniques to help Oriana manage her emotions and reactions. These practices align with spiritual principles of self-control and seeking forgiveness. We use positive reinforcement to acknowledge and reward Oriana's positive behaviors. This encourages her to embrace her new identity and strengthen her spiritual faith. We facilitate opportunities for Oriana to build healthy relationships with peers and authority figures, emphasizing the importance of forgiveness and compassion, as taught in the religious texts.

Through a combination of evidence-based interventions and spiritual guidance, Oriana's behavior gradually transforms. She learns to regulate her emotions, build healthy relationships, and find comfort in her faith. Our aim should be to help Oriana not only navigate the challenges of her past trauma but also to instill in her the spiritual values of love, compassion, and resilience.

Sam's Anger

Sam, an 11th-grade student, has been displaying severe anger issues in both verbal and physical forms. His outbursts and aggression have raised concerns among teachers, fellow students, and his family. Surprisingly, there is no apparent history of trauma or significant adverse life events. Sam's anger issues seem to emerge without a clear underlying cause. His frequent outbursts and aggressive behavior have disrupted the learning environment, strained relationships, and negatively impacted his overall well-being. As a religious psychologist, I believe that the teachings of spirituality can offer valuable guidance and support for Sam's transformation. We initiate a journey of self-control and spiritual growth with Sam. By exploring Sam's moral principles (which may or may not spring from a distinct religious background), we emphasize the importance of self-discipline, patience, and prayer in managing anger. "For the Spirit God gave us does not make us timid, but gives us power, love, and self-discipline." (2 Timothy 1:7, KJV)

Sam is guided toward forgiveness and reconciliation. He is encouraged to understand the power of forgiveness to release anger and promote healing and reconciliation in his relationships. We introduce the concepts of love and compassion, emphasizing their role in recovery and fostering positive relationships. Sam learns that love and compassion can be powerful tools in managing anger. To help Sam manage his rage, we introduce mindfulness and emotional regulation techniques. Through prayer and reflection, he learns to cultivate peace, gentleness, and self-control, aligning with the religious teachings.

Sam's anger issues begin to recede through a combination of spiritual growth, self-control, forgiveness, love, and mindfulness. Sam learns to recognize and manage his emotions more effectively and finds healing and reconciliation in his relationships. We aim to help Sam overcome his anger and instill the spiritual values of love, compassion, and forgiveness, promoting spiritual and emotional well-being.

Chapter 17:

THE UNVEILING: A JOURNEY OF HEALING & HOPE

There are endless strategies waiting to be explored in behavior management; our mission is to discover the one that resonates with each student's unique journey.

    Christin's journey was not without hardships, but her unwavering faith became a beacon of hope, guiding her through life's darkest storms. As she navigated the challenges that life had thrown her way, her faith in God became a constant source of strength and solace.

    After her tumultuous childhood, Christin's path was marked by uncertainty and adversity. The scars of her early trauma manifested in her teenage years as she struggled with mental health issues, behavior problems, and a deep sense of hopelessness. She had no home, just a stream of foster families that made her feel she was a burden; she was broken and anger and resentment consumed her.

    It was during this challenging phase that Christin found her way back to her faith. She began attending a local church, where she discovered a supportive community that embraced her openly. She delved into the teachings of the Bible, finding comfort in verses that spoke of strength in the face of adversity, such as Psalm 46:1-3 – "God is our refuge and strength, an ever-present help in trouble. Therefore we will not fear, though the earth give way and the mountains fall," and Isaiah 41:10, "So do not fear, for I am with you; do not be dismayed, for I am your God. I will strengthen you and help you; I will uphold you with my righteous right hand" (KJV).

Christin's journey towards healing and transformation wasn't instantaneous. She sought therapy and counseling, addressing her post-traumatic stress disorder, clinical depression, anxiety, and intermittent explosive disorder. It was in these therapeutic sessions that her faith became a powerful tool for self-discovery and recovery. Through Cognitive Behavioral Therapy (CBT), mindfulness, and meditation, she began challenging negative thought patterns and managing her anxiety. Her faith, combined with these therapeutic techniques, provided a sturdy foundation for her journey to wholeness. Christin's commitment and reliance on God were evident in every aspect of her life. She started to use her experiences to help others who were going through similar challenges, sharing her story and offering support and encouragement to those in need. She volunteered at her church, mentoring troubled youth and leading support groups.

Christin fondly recollects the ritual of dressing up every Sunday to accompany her grandmother to church when she was younger. Those cherished memories of attending church with her grandmother resonated deeply with her. Her grandmother had imparted invaluable wisdom, emphasizing the significance of unwavering trust in God during life's most challenging moments. However, when her grandmother passed away, Christin believed that those teachings had faded into her past. Having faced the turmoil of her childhood and the emotional scars it left, she began to understand the need for faith and hope. The adversity she had experienced gave her a unique perspective on resilience and the transformative power of faith.

Now as a 35-year-old, Christin has come a long way from the troubled teenager she once was. Her faith continues to be the cornerstone of her life. Today, she serves as a dedicated social worker, a calling she wholeheartedly embraces. In this role, she tirelessly advocates for mental health awareness and stands as a pillar of support for individuals with similar challenges. Christin's life is a testament to her determination to shift her mindset in order to change the negative behavior. Her transformation has not only positively impacted her own life, but it has also inspired countless individuals on their own path to healing.

Today, Christin serves as hope, a living testament to the power of faith and the possibility of redemption and healing. Her journey reminds us that even in the darkest of times, one can find their way back to the light, guided by their faith and the belief that, with God, all things are possible.

Final Thoughts

"God's Word" encompasses His teachings and spiritual guidance in various religious texts, influencing how individuals interact with the world and shape their behavior. These texts offer a framework for conducting oneself ethically and with integrity, emphasizing love, compassion, and humility. While individuals who follow these teachings may endeavor to align their behavior with their spiritual beliefs, it is essential to acknowledge the diversity of interpretations within different religious communities. Personal beliefs, cultural contexts, and the influence of religious leaders all play a substantial role in how these teachings are understood and applied. By embracing open-minded discussions and recognizing these factors, we can appreciate the rich perspectives that enrich our communities and our understanding of spirituality's role in shaping behavior.

I firmly believe in the impact of spirituality on our lives, especially in the challenging field of education. The incorporation of spirituality into our approach to behavior management can have a transformative effect on students, helping them develop into compassionate, responsible individuals. This book has explored the power of spirituality in helping adults make a mindset shift and ultimately shaping behavior. We have highlighted five key areas of spirituality that have a significant role.

Yet, I would be remiss if I did not recognize that spirituality is deeply personal, and its influence on behavior can vary widely from person to person. While it can potentially bring about positive change, it can also be misinterpreted and misused to justify harmful actions. A comprehensive understanding of the broader context and other factors influencing behavior is essential.

In our ever-changing world, where the teaching profession faces numerous challenges, tapping into spiritual resources can guide and sustain us in our work with students. I hope this book sparked valuable discussions and exploration within the educational community about the influence of mindsets and spirituality on behavior.

The journey of shaping behavior is complex and nuanced, influenced by individual differences and the specific contexts in which it occurs. There is no one-size-fits-all approach, but the wisdom and guidance provided by spiritual teachings can play a role in creating a foundation. By embracing the values of love, compassion, and forgiveness, we can not only support our students but also foster a more harmonious and just society. As educators of faith, we are responsible for harnessing the power of spirituality for the betterment of ourselves and the generations we nurture.

References

Abu-Nimer, Mohammed; Katalin Nelson, Renáta. (2021). *Evaluating interreligious peacebuilding and dialogue.* De Gruyter. Retrieved from https://doi.org/10.1515/9783110624625

Bogusław Milerski & Tadeusz J. Zieliński (2023) Religion in a world-view neutral school. Challenges on the example of Poland, *British Journal of Religious Education,* 45 (3), 288-300.

Bunting, Victoria H. (2020). The effects of positive student-teacher relationships on students' perceptions of school safety. *Educational Specialist,* (Current), 3.

Caleon, I. S., Ilham, N. Q. B., Ong, C. L., & Tan, J. P.-L. (2019). Cascading effects of gratitude: a sequential mediation analysis of gratitude, interpersonal relationships, school resilience and school well-being, *Asia-Pacific Education Researcher.* 28(4), 303–312.

Cerqueira Rodrigues, M. A., Campos Barbosa, F., Dias Lopes, G. C., Santacroce, L., & Pereira Lopes, P. C. (2023). Intersection between Spirituality and Neuroscience: Biological Bases of

Transcendental Experiences. Environmental & Social Management Journal / Revista de Gestão Social e Ambiental, 17(9), 1–8.

Cho H, Ryu S, Noh J, Lee J. (2016). The effectiveness of daily Mindful Breathing Practices on Test Anxiety of Students. PLOS One. Oct 20;11(10):e0164822. doi: 10.1371/journal.pone.0164822.

Cook, Clayton & Coco, Susanna & Zhang, Yanchen & Fiat, Aria & Duong, Mylien & Renshaw, Tyler & Long, Anna & Frank, Sophia. (2018). Cultivating positive teacher–student relationships: preliminary evaluation of the stablish–maintain – restore (EMR) method. *School Psychology Review,* 47.

D'Alessandro, A. M., Butterfield, K. M., Hanceroglu, L., & Roberts, K. P. (2022). Listen to the children: elementary school students' perspectives on a mindfulness intervention. *Journal of Child & Family Studies,* 31(8), 2108–2120.

Darling-Hammond, S., Ruiz, M., Eberhardt, J. L., & Okonofua, J. A. (2023). The dynamic nature of student discipline and discipline disparities. *Proceedings of the National Academy of Sciences of the United States of America,* 120(17), 1–10. https://doi.org/10.1073/pnas.2120417120

Devine PG, Forscher PS, Austin AJ, Cox WT. (2012). Long-term reduction in implicit race bias: A prejudice habit-breaking intervention. *Journal of Experimental Social Psychology* (JESP).Nov;48(6)

Filter, Kevin & Michelle E. Alvarez. (2012). *Functional behavioral assessment: A three-tiered prevention model.* Oxford University Press.

Firpo-Cappiello, R. (2020). Retrain Your Brain: Cognitive behavioral therapy may be an effective and safe way to manage migraine and symptoms of other neurologic disorders by changing the way you think about them. Brain & Life, 16(1), 36–37.

Giuliani F, Cannito L, Gigliotti G, Rosa A, Pietroni D, Palumbo R. (2023). The joint effect of framing and defaults on choice behavior. *Psychology Research.* Jun;87(4):1114-1128. doi: 10.1007/s 00426- 0 22-01726-3. Epub 2022 Sep 5. PMID: 36063226; PMCID: PMC10192178.

Glenna M. Billingsley, Jennifer M. McKenzie & Brenda K.

Scheuermann. (2020). The effects of a structured classroom management system in secondary resource classrooms. *Exceptionality.* 28(5), 317-332, DOI: 10.1080/09362835. 2018.1522257

Goralnik, L., & Marcus, S. (2020). Resilient learners, learning resilience: Contemplative practice in the sustainability classroom. *New Directions for Teaching & Learning.* (161), 83–99. https://doi.org/10.1002/tl.20375

Grayson, J. L., & Alvarez, H. K. (2008). School climate factors relating to teacher burnout: A mediator model. *Teaching and Teacher Education.* 24(5), 1349-1363.

Hamric, Ann B., and Lucia D. Wocial. (2016). Institutional ethics resources: Creating moral spaces. *Hastings Center Report.* https://doi.org/10.1002/hast.627.

Hayes, S. C., Strosahl, K. D., & Wilson, K. G. (2016). *Acceptance and commitment therapy: The process and practice of mindful change (2nd ed.)*. Guilford Press.

Hidayah, R., Mu'awanah, E., Zamhari, A., Munardji, & Naqiyah. (2021). Learning worship as a way to improve students' discipline, motivation, and achievement at school. *Journal of Ethnic and Cultural Studies.* 8(3), 292–310.

Higgins, J. P., Riggleman, S., & Lohmann, M. J. (2023). A Practical Guide to Writing Behavior Intervention Plans for Young Children. https://core.ac.uk/download/553027199.pdf

Honsinger, C., & Brown, M. H. (2019). Preparing trauma-sensitive teachers: Strategies for teacher educators. Teacher Educators' Journal, 12, 129-152. National Child Traumatic Stress Network Schools Committee. (2008, October). Child trauma toolkit for educators. Los, Angeles, CA & Durham, NC: National Center for Child Traumatic Stress

Kaspar, K. L., & Massey, S. L. (2023). Implementing social-emotional learning in the elementary classroom. *Early Childhood Education Journal.* 51(4), 641–650. https://doi.org/10.1007/s10643-022-01324-3

King, R. B. (2020). Mindsets are contagious: The social contagion of implicit theories of intelligence among classmates. *The British Journal of Educational Psychology.* 90(2), 349–363. https://doi.org/10.1111/bjep.12285

King James Bible. (2017). King James Bible Online. https://www.kingjamesbibleonline.org/ (Original work published 1769)

Kirby, James. (2020). Nurturing Family Environments for Children: Compassion-Focused Parenting as a Form of Parenting Intervention. Education Sciences. 2020; 10(1):3.

Lodi, E., Perrella, L., Lepri, G. L., Scarpa, M. L., & Patrizi, P. (2022). Use of restorative justice and restorative practices at school: A systematic literature review. *International Journal of Environmental Research and Public Health*. 19(1). https://doi.org/10.3390/ijerph19010096

Lupu, Ira, F. Elwood, E. Davis, D. Masci at Pew Research Center Religion in the public schools Mirams, L., et al. October 2019. Brief body-scan meditation practice improves somatosensory perceptual decision-making. *Consciousness and Cognition* (2012)

Martin RE, Ochsner KN. (*2016*). The neuroscience of emotion regulation development: Implications for Education. *Current Opinion in Behavioral Sciences*. Aug;10:142-148.

Mathur, S. R., & Corley, K. M. (2014). Bringing ethics into the classroom: Making a case for frameworks, multiple perspectives and narrative sharing. *International Education Studies.* 7(9), 136–147.

Matsumoto, David & Juang, Linda. (2017). *Culture and Psychology image 6th edition.*

Maynard BR, Farina A, Dell NA, Kelly MS. (2019). Effects of trauma-informed approaches in schools: A systematic review. Campbell Systematic Reviews. Jul 17;15(1-2):e1018. doi: 10.1002/cl2.1018. PMID: 37131480; PMCID: PMC8356508.

Ministry of Education. (2013). Supporting minds : An educator's guide to promoting students' mental health and well-being (Draft version).

Moss, W. L., & Moses, D. A. (2018). *Frustration tolerance: Raising independent, self-confident kids: Nine essential skills to teach your child or teen.* American Psychological Association. https://doi.org/10.1037/0000067-000

Murakami, Rose & Campos, Claudinei José Gomes. (2012) Religion and mental health: the challenge of integrating religiosity to patient care. Revista Brasileira de Enfermagem, v. 65, n. 2, p. 361-367

NAEYC. (2020). Developmentally Appropriate Practice [Position Statement]

Mullen, J. D. (2006). Nature, Nurture, and Individual Change. Behavior and Philosophy, 34, 1–17.

Nalipay, M. J. N., King, R. B., Mordeno, I. G., Chai, C.-S., & Jong, M. S. (2021). Teachers with a growth mindset are motivated and engaged: the relationships among mindsets, motivation, and engagement in teaching. *Social Psychology of Education.* 24(6), 1663–1684.

Pong, H.-K., & Lam, P. (2023). The effect of service learning on the development of trait emotional intelligence and adversity quotient in youths: An experimental study. *International Journal of Environmental Research and Public Health.* 20(6).

Purpose & Principles. MindSet Safety Management. (2023, October 4). https://mindsetinstructortraining.com/guiding-principles/

Romani, P. W., Luehring, M. C., Hays, T. M., & Boorse, A. L. (2023). Comparisons of functional behavior assessment procedures to the functional analysis of problem behavior. *Behavior Analysis: Research and Practice.* 23(1), 36–48. https://doi.org/10.1037/bar0000258.supp (Supplemental)

Rutten BPF, Hammels C, Geschwind N, Menne-Lothmann C, Pishva E, Schruers K, van den Hove D, Kenis G, van Os J, Wichers (2013) Resilience in mental health: linking psychological and neurobiological perspectives, Acta Psychiatrica Scandinavica. 128: 3–20

Scheffel, T.-L., & Hives, L. (2021). Shifting mindsets about educating young children. *Learning Professional.* 42(2), 26–29.

Sholikhah, Z., Wang, X. and Li, W. (2019), The role of spiritual leadership in fostering discretionary behaviors: The mediating effect of organization-based self-esteem and workplace spirituality. *International Journal of Law and Management.* Vol. 61 No. 1, pp. 232-249.

Taren, A. A., Gianaros, P. J., Greco, C. M., Lindsay, E. K., Fairgrieve, A., Brown, K. W., Rosen, R. K., Ferris, J. L., Julson, E., Marsland, A. L., Bursley, J. K., Ramsburg, J., &

Creswell, J. D. (2015). Mindfulness meditation training alters stress-related amygdala resting state functional connectivity: A randomized controlled trial. *Social Cognitive and Affective Neuroscience.* 10(12), 1758–1768.

Thalén, P. 2021. "World View Instead of Religion?" In O. Franck and P. Thalén (Eds), *Religious Education in a Post-Secular Age. Case Studies from Europe.* 157–178. Cham: Palgrave Macmillan.

Springer Nature Switzerland. What is the amendment about prayer in public schools? https://www.kembrel.com/writing-101/what-is-the-amendment-about-prayer-in-public-schools/

The Torah (3rd ed.). (2015). The Jewish Publication Society. (Original work published 1962).

Walls, Therapist Scott, (2017), *Behavior Management Skills for Classroom Success.* (2017). Video/DVD. PESI Inc.: Eau Claire, WI. Retrieved from https://video.alexanderstreet.com/watch/behavior-management-skills-for-classroom-success

Webster EM. The Impact of Adverse Childhood Experiences on Health and Development in Young Children. Glob Pediatr Health. 2022 Feb 26;9:2333794X221078708. doi: 10.1177/2333794X221078708. PMID: 35237713; PMCID: PMC8882933.

Zimmerman, K. N., Torelli, J. N., & Chow, J. C. (2022). Planning positive reinforcement cycles in behavior intervention plans. Behavior Analysis in Practice, 15(3), 924–937. https://doi.org/10.1007/s40617-021-00663-8

ABOUT THE AUTHOR

Regina Christian Massey is a proud native of Atlanta, Georgia, with deep roots in the local educational landscape. She is an educator, instructional leader, and advocate committed to supporting whole-child development through trauma-aware, evidence-based, and faith-informed practices. With professional experience spanning education, behavior support, and instructional coaching, she brings a compassionate and practical perspective to understanding behavior in children and adolescents.

Regina's work focuses on helping educators, parents, and helping professionals move beyond surface-level behavior management toward approaches that prioritize emotional regulation, accountability, restoration, and growth. Through her leadership with Teacher Mod Squad, she supports schools and educators in building inclusive, responsive learning environments grounded in research, reflection, and ethical practice.

Although her latest work is informed by a Christian worldview, Regina emphasizes respect for diverse beliefs and professional boundaries, offering strategies that are applicable across faith-based and secular settings alike. Her writing bridges theory and real-world application, empowering readers to respond to behavior with clarity, empathy, and purpose.

www.ingramcontent.com/pod-product-compliance
Lightning Source LLC
LaVergne TN
LVHW052257070426
835507LV00036B/3301